From Hell to Breakfast in Old Montana

A True Saga

LELAND BLANCHARD

ISBN: 1548434175
ISBN 13: 9781548434175
Library of Congress Control Number: 2017910290
CreateSpace Independent Publishing Platform
North Charleston, South Carolina

CONTENTS

CREDIT WHERE CREDIT'S DUE

I've used pseudonyms for the book's two principal sources, who also figure in the narrative itself. They are James Vidmar and Danis Vidmar (see the Introduction). They made the book possible.

An important source was the weekly *Roundup Record*, founded in 1908 by A.W. Eiselein. The chapter "From Drought to Dementia" is based on the paper's superb coverage of a 1930 murder case. I thank the *Roundup Record-Tribune & Winnett Times* for permission to reprint material.

I stumbled across a treasure trove in the form of research by the late John F. Taylor, an employee of the Bureau of Land Management (BLM). Back in 1990 he wrote an amazing report for a coworker who wanted to know more about homesteading ancestor Martin Brodar. When I visited the BLM office in Billings, those who knew Taylor had no idea where he'd dug up such highly detailed information. They praised his work record and, in this case, his investigative skills. I like to think he'd be pleased to see his hard work find an audience. This material is featured in the chapter "Long Road to a Dead End."

A great big thanks to Danis's daughter-in-law Earline, of Townsend, Montana, who had produced a genealogy of the Vidmars of Slovenia long before I entered the scene. Earline was also helpful in trying to unravel mysteries involving the clan.

And a great big thanks to Karen Brattain, of Portland, Oregon, an editor of books and academic periodicals. The heavily marked-up, typewritten manuscript had rested in a drawer for years when I met Karen by chance. What luck that Karen was willing to help bring this project to fruition. Otherwise it might still be snoozing in that drawer.

INTRODUCTION: BRINGING GHOSTS BACK TO LIFE

This book is about folks History was wont to forget when the tombstones went up. I first heard of them from a coworker at the *Billings Gazette* back in 1976. This friend, whom I will call James Vidmar (not his real name), never tired of talking about his grandparents and others who'd been around during Montana's last gasp of pioneering.

I envied James because he'd grown up among genuine pioneers, South Slav immigrants whose lives were much like those of pioneers from the far distant past. James thus grew up at a time and place that straddled two eras.

No sooner had I suggested he write a book about these people than I left Montana after only a year. I never thought I'd return, but I did, in retirement, twenty-four years later. Once again, James regaled me with those ghosts from his past. Had he not done so, this book never would have materialized.

I plunged into the project, and James and I spent many days visiting old-timers to learn what we could about the book's main characters.

The other essential source was James's uncle Danis Vidmar, last survivor of his immediate family. At our first meeting, he was guarded with me. But over time, he came to regard me as a friend and provided amazing details about the book's principal figures, himself included.

Still, I faced major hurdles, since many ghosts had taken some secrets to the grave. It wasn't always easy trying to fill in the blanks, and I often felt more like a sleuth than a writer. But after sixteen years tooling with this material, I'm confident in the way I filled in the blanks and connected the dots.

If I have erred at times, it is with minor matters. All the major dramatic events happened as I've presented them. I didn't invent or embellish anything. What little dialogue there is happens to be genuine. And the two astonishing letters in the chapter "Heart of Darkness" are presented verbatim, replete with grammatical and spelling errors.

To protect the privacy of descendants, I changed the names of all but a few minor characters. In any case, some name changes were necessary for another reason; South Slavs back in the day were excessively fond of names such as Frank and Mary, Ann and Anton. Some shared not only first names but last names too, which would have made it a chore for readers to keep track of who was who.

This multigenerational account, I think, presents a rare look at the downside of coal camp and homestead life in south-central Montana, with the city of Roundup as principal backdrop.

If those ghosts could rise from the grave, how amazed they'd be to see that History hadn't forgotten them at all. On the other hand, some would surely be shocked senseless and hotter than hell to read of their misdeeds.

1

BATTLE-AX BARA

No one would remember how Bara Stupak got her hooks into hapless teenager Ania Mazur. But this wily schemer hooked her, all right, as easily as reeling in a baby trout. Soon after they met, in a Pennsylvania coal camp, Bara took her by train to a remote coal camp in Montana, where two of Bara's brothers worked. It spelled doom for Ania, who was like a fish out of water in that rugged world.

The year was 1913.

Bara Stupak, at age twenty-six, had just sailed to America with nine-year-old son Rudi. Husband Matt, a coal miner, remained in Germany. Bara's mission was to find a suitable coal camp in Pennsylvania where the Slovenian family might settle down. She would then visit her brothers in Montana. It was a long-drawn-out affair, spending a week at sea in steerage then being processed at New York's Ellis Island, which could take hours, even days.

Single women with offspring were turned away if they lacked any source of income and someone didn't step up to the plate at Ellis and take responsibility. This raises the question of how Bara entered the country with Rudi. She gave officials not her married name, Stupak, but her maiden name, Vidmar. That suggests that brother Merlin Vidmar not only met her at Ellis but that Bara presented herself as his wife. What supports this notion is that when Matt Stupak immigrated the following year, he told Ellis officials he would stay with his "sister," Bara Vidmar, in Pennsylvania.

That Bara came over ahead of Matt seems unusual. She certainly was her own woman. She knew what she wanted at an early age, running away from home at sixteen, following Matt from Slovenia to Germany, and bearing his son out of wedlock. But she definitely was Mrs. Stupak when she arrived at Ellis, not Miss or Mrs. Vidmar.

If Merlin did meet her at Ellis, he likely headed back to Montana while Bara toured various coal camps in Pennsylvania. That she didn't know English wouldn't have been a huge obstacle since she spoke German, and Germans were the biggest ethnic group not only in Pennsylvania but in the United States as well. Also, at least one coal camp outside Pittsburgh had several hundred Slovenians.

As for Ania Mazur, she'd immigrated with family from Poland in 1909, when she was thirteen. Her father was a miner, and they settled in a coal camp at Ambler, just north of Philadelphia. An unschooled peasant, Ania had never learned to read and write, and her English was poor after four years. At seventeen, she was surprisingly childlike in looks and behavior, with quirky habits, such as donning her nicest frocks when doing messy household chores.

When and how she met Bara Stupak is a mystery. In the decades after Ania's premature death, no descendant had a handle on who or what had brought Ania to Montana. Her eldest son thought maybe an older brother had taken her, but Ania had no older brother. And she certainly hadn't forged out on her own. Luckily, there was one invaluable source, Merlin's stepdaughter Julia Virga, who said time and again before her death at ninety-six that Bara Stupak definitely brought Ania to the coal camp of Klein, Montana.

The likelihood is that Bara met the Mazur family while touring coal country.

Also mysterious is why Bara wanted to take Ania to Montana so soon after meeting her. Or why Ania would want to go. Or why the Mazurs allowed it at all.

Bara's action suggests she took an immediate liking to Ania, and a good guess is that it's because this sprite-like child was a cutie with much charm. She probably was on the order of five feet tall, plump, with a smile to melt the heart. She wasn't pretty by conventional standards, endowed with a too-prominent nose and chin. But the bee-stung lips and oddly Asiatic eyes made up for any shortcomings.

But Bara's real motivation may have been to secure a possible wife for kid brother Luka. After three years in the Klein coal camp, neither brother had found a bride. After all, single women were as scarce as hens' teeth. Merlin, however, had become enamored with a woman whose husband was terminally ill.

The Mazurs' motivation may have been their fear that Ania, due to what appeared to be a learning disability, might become a lifelong burden. As for Ania's motivation, her childlike spirit may have welcomed the chance to visit a land far, far away.

Perhaps Bara was also upbeat about the possibility of Ania working in the Klein boardinghouse, where her brothers lived. If nothing worked out, Bara could always bring Ania back on her return trip.

■ ■ ■

When our party of three reached Chicago, they boarded a Milwaukee Road train that took them to Roundup, Montana. Before the coal boom, it had been known only as the site of a huge cattle roundup each fall, an event that had started four decades back. At the time of Custer's Last Stand, in 1876, about a hundred miles south, cowpokes calmly grazed their cattle all along the Musselshell River Valley. Although the Indian Wars were still raging throughout the West, one would never have known it in sleepy Roundup, where serenity reigned in the shadows of the rugged Bull Mountains.

The train that carried Bara, Rudi, and Ania to Roundup was running on a new route that had begun service four years back. It was the Milwaukee's Pacific Extension, America's last transcontinental route, connecting Chicago with the Puget Sound. Roundup was included in the route only because it had the coal to refuel the trains at the midway point. Because Roundup was a few miles south of the route, the tiny hamlet pulled up stakes and relocated right alongside the tracks.

Republic Coal, a Milwaukee subsidiary, dug a mine just south of New Roundup, on the south side of the Musselshell River. But after five years of operation, the slant-shaft mine was abandoned in 1912 due to flooding. Engineers settled on a place a little more to the south, land owned by Marcus Klein, a Slovenian immigrant who became one of the movers and shakers in newly formed Musselshell County (1911). The deep-shaft mine was a huge undertaking, and when it opened the camp was a tent city until the company could build houses. It was a hardship post, which is why Republic sought workers from overseas. The greatest numbers who heeded the call were South Slavs. This is where Bara's brothers, Merlin and Luka, worked.

The mine triggered a boom in New Roundup. By 1913, the Old West of legend may have faded into history, but not in Roundup. It was the Wild West all over again, with buildings sprouting faster than mushrooms in a rainforest. Thousands of fortune seekers piled into this raw outpost, bringing along all the pathologies of humankind, with crimes such as a mass murder on a farm south of town and a slaying in which a young man killed his mother with an ax on a street in broad daylight. Adding to the problem was liquor, which flowed like a river, with a whopping seventy saloons in the new county.

Another impetus to Roundup's growth was passage of the Enlarged Homestead Act of 1909, which brought thousands of farm families to the area. On December 24, 1909, the weekly *Roundup Record* offered this Christmas cheer to business folk:

> The Milwaukee exhibit car of Montana (agriculture), which
> is now making a tour of Iowa, is creating a great deal of
> interest. ... The car will undoubtedly be the cause of an
> immigration next year of considerable magnitude.

Roundup sits on the north flank of the Bull Mountains, where the tallest ridge falls just short of five thousand feet—fifteen hundred if one subtracts the land's base elevation. The Bulls provide an impressive backdrop to Roundup's flat landscape. North, east, and west of town, as far as the eye can see, is gently rolling grassland, grass that once fed the mighty buffalo herds. Ancient indigenous Americans called the mountains the Bulls because the basin was a popular hangout for the herds.

Threading its way eastward through the mountains is the Musselshell River, so named by the Lewis and Clark Expedition because of the plethora of shoreline mussels. It's a humble river that winds through the valley like a harmless serpent, pitiably reduced to a series of puddles during exceptionally hot, dry summers. But during heavy spring rains, it can morph into a raging anaconda, swallowing anything along its path.

■ ■ ■

Upon arrival at Roundup's train depot, Bara Stupak hired a wagoner for the three-and-a-half-mile trip to Klein, since wagons were the standard form of public transportation between Roundup and Klein at the time. Some miners who lived in Roundup commuted on bicycles.

One wonders how Bara, Ania, and Rudi responded to a landscape so radically different from heavily forested Eastern Europe, Slovenia being one of the greenest places on the continent. Here they saw vegetation they'd never seen before, from small flowering cacti to groves of sagebrush. While the plains are bereft of trees, at least the slopes of the Bulls are festooned with pygmy ponderosas, testament to the region's low rainfall, less than fourteen inches a year on average.

Bara led the way into the company boardinghouse, and what a pleasure it must have been to converse in her own language with Slovenian husband-and-wife managers Martin and Maria Meznarik. Bara, who spoke up for Ania, had no trouble convincing the Meznariks that her sweet-faced companion would make a fine worker.

Bara would have known right away that, despite the presence of South Slavs, Klein was not the place for her, Matt, and Rudi. It was a hardship post, plain and simple. Company houses, situated chockablock on both sides of a coulee, had only four rooms and lacked running water and electricity. Communal privies and wells were standard. There was a big company store that offered groceries and dry goods, a post office, saloon, amusement hall, and not much else. Bara had already decided that the coal-rich area of Pittsburgh, Pennsylvania, was a more sensible place to sink roots. Plus there were a great many Slovenians in the coal camps there.

Bara's stay at the boardinghouse was productive in a way she never could have expected. She learned much about running a boardinghouse, and in Cheswick, Pennsylvania, she and her second husband would buy and operate one.

Maria Meznarik soon became greatly disappointed with Ania's work. Julia Virga, Maria's niece, remembered her aunt complaining about the problems she had with the girl: "I had to teach her everything!"

Being young, single, and a cutie to boot, vulnerable Ania was like a hen in a fox den, surrounded day and night by dozens of randy young boardinghouse miners. Luka, however, was not interested. The "fox" who moved in quickly for the "kill" had an edge over competitors since he was Polish and spoke Ania's language. Kamil Balinski, who'd been in America for a decade, had three things in common with Luka: he too was antisocial, was a compulsive womanizer, and had zero interest in marriage.

There was more than a whiff of sleaze in Balinski's makeup. Before coming to Klein he'd bummed around the country, working here and there, riding the rails in boxcars with other bums. Unlike Luka, however, he was anything but handsome, being of medium height and slight build. Because of his small stature, he'd feared being mugged during the many times he stayed in hobo camps, or "jungles." But his seedy nature wouldn't have been apparent to Ania since at age twenty-eight he had the clean-cut looks of an altar boy.

■ ■ ■

Eight years younger than Merlin, Luka took his cues from his brother, who had a lot more backbone. One can tell this from the only photo in which they are seen together. Luka looks quite callow at twenty-two, while

Merlin seems so mature at thirty that the brother could be the father. Merlin comes across as stalwart, disciplined, responsible, focused. Luka seems just the opposite: a sullen and bored young punk.

Luka may have been the black sheep in their peasant family at Celje, Slovenia (part of Austria until the end of World War One). There were plenty of "sheep" in the family—sixteen children in all—and the father, Mike, picked on Luka a lot. In later life only Luka complained about his father's cruelty, how he would beat the daylights out of him, oddly, after returning home from Sunday services at the Catholic church. The abuse was so bad it turned Luka into an atheist, for he felt a loving God would not tolerate such violence. Ironically, after marriage, Luka would prove he was a chip off the old block.

Luka and his father weren't the only violent Vidmars. Merlin was a Jekyll and Hyde whose wicked potion was booze. When sober he was kind and loving. But when drunk he was as dangerous as a grizzly. If his fists didn't suffice to win an argument, he might grab a gun or an ax.

A big difference between the brothers is that Merlin wasn't a lazybones like Luka. He was the first to leave his peasant family, becoming a coal miner in Caldbeck, Germany. Then, after hearing about the Klein mine, he sailed to America on the *Kroonland* in June 1910. Six months later, he sent for Luka, paying all expenses.

■ ■ ■

It was through Merlin's relationship with Louise, the sister of the boardinghouse wife-manager, that he learned something that would have been hush-hush in that day and age, especially in a camp populated by so many Catholics. Ania was pregnant. Martin and Maria Meznarik must have been in a dither over what to do. Marriage was the last thing Kamil Balinski wanted out of life, and Ania had no friends or relatives to turn to. And she could hardly keep her job with a baby in tow.

Louise's daughter Julia Virga, interviewed at age ninety-two, said Luka "stole" Ania from Kamil. But when reminded that evidence didn't support that, she backed down. Anyway, she was a toddler when these events took place. Moreover, as Merlin's stepdaughter (briefly), she came to hate him and his brother with a passion and had wanted to see Luka as thief. One thing is certain: if Luka "stole" Ania, Kamil abetted him in the theft. Kamil not only absconded for parts unknown—he was neither seen nor heard from again.

The only plausible scenario is that Merlin or Bara, acting singly or together, pushed their kid brother into a marriage he didn't want at all. Merlin, who seemed kind of a father figure to Luka, probably took the more active hand. Twice more, as we will see, would he play matchmaker. He was a busybody who liked to meddle in the lives of kin. Although his intentions were good, his judgment was terrible.

Luka was easily the worst marital candidate in the camp, if not the entire county. Not only was he a loner with an explosive temper, he was also a compulsive womanizer with no interest at all in being a husband and father. Both he and Merlin consorted with prostitutes. Moreover, he was not very bright, and he was notoriously lazy. He actually worked only when he felt like it or when strapped for cash. Such an arrangement was okay with Republic, which paid workers for how much coal they shoveled on any given day.

The marriage of Luka Vidmar and Ania Mazur was truly a match made in hell.

■ ■ ■

Bara Stupak didn't stick around for the civil service wedding in Roundup on January 31, 1914, when Ania was three months pregnant. She and Rudi headed back to Pennsylvania, and she located a rental unit in the town of Claridge, near Pittsburgh.

The following May, husband Matt arrived at Ellis Island. Paperwork shows he was thirty-three years old, five-foot-eight, fair skinned, bald, with only $35 to his name. Asked about his destination, he said (as was noted earlier) that he would join his "sister" in Claridge.

The marriage must have existed in name only, because for the next seven years, Bara and Rudi made trips each year to Roundup. Bara bought a house near the fairgrounds, and teenage Rudi worked as a track layer at Coal Camp No. 3, just outside of town.

But those visits were hardly peaceful idylls since the Vidmars and Stupaks were beset by tragedy. Three years into the Luka-Ania marriage this item appeared in the *Roundup Record*:

> The little eighteen months old child of Mr. and Mrs. Luka Vidmar met death in a terrible way last Saturday. The child sat down in a pan of scalding grease which his mother had set just outside the door to cool after having cooked a goose in it. How the child got to the grease is unknown, but it was terribly burned and suffered terribly until Monday when it passed away. The funeral was held Wednesday and the body was buried in the Old Roundup Cemetery under the supervision of Undertaker Action.

Luka Jr. was the couple's second child. The death certificate stated that the boiler held scalding water, not grease.

Tragedy struck again two years later, when Merlin's wife, Louise, died of tuberculosis after only five years of marriage. Her two young daughters from her previous marriage, Ann and Julia, were turned over to her relatives.

Then in 1921 Bara Stupak suffered what may have been the greatest emotional blow of her life.

From the *Roundup Record*:

> Rudolph Stupak, 16, who lives near the Roundup Mercantile company's store in West Roundup, was drowned while playing in the Musselshell River near the bridge to the fairgrounds on Sunday afternoon. The boy was recovered shortly afterwards but all efforts at resuscitation failed.
>
> Young Stupak, who was employed at the No. 3 mine, was in the river with several other young men and no one knew he was in trouble until after his body had disappeared from view for some time. It had been under water

nearly half an hour when recovered. Dr. W.I. Firey was called and he used the fire department's pulmotor unsuccessfully in order to bring back the spark of life.

No one would remember the extent of Bara's grief, but they did so her titanic fury. Fury? An odd reaction to the loss of a son by drowning. But Bara was furious, all right, a fury that eclipsed her grief. So much so that she refused to attend the funeral! It was because Rudi had defied her orders: *You are never to swim in that river!* Bara even refused to buy a headstone for what ended up being the boy's unmarked grave in Old Roundup Cemetery.

A month later still another tragic occurrence took place, and it appeared in the *Roundup Record* not as a news story but as a one-paragraph advertisement:

> A small house belonging to Mrs. Stupak near the Pavilion was burned yesterday afternoon. The fire department responded promptly, but the flames had attained such headway that all efforts to save the building were futile. The house and contents are a total loss, partly covered by insurance. Don't forget! Insurance before the fire is insurance after the fire. Insurance for everyman and everything. Mark D. Dearborn, 125 Main St.

Somehow the fire seems suspicious, coming so soon after Rudi's death. Did Bara undergo a psychotic meltdown and torch the place due to intense grief and anger? Whatever, she soon left Roundup, never to return. Not even when Ania Vidmar died, five years later, in 1926. At least that's the opinion of Ania's fifth-born son, Danis, who was two months shy of his sixth birthday when his mom died. But Danis, as we'll soon learn, had remarkably good recall, even in his late eighties. If Bara had come for the funeral, Danis would have remembered. Had she come, she likely would have felt required to watch over the six children for a time. She'd done exactly that for Merlin's stepdaughters when Louise died.

There's a strong probability Bara stayed away because she didn't want to be dragged into a situation in which she might have been expected to provide a home for one or more of the children. Everyone knew Luka would not keep them. They were soon parceled out to foster homes.

Bara by then had her own agenda, and it precluded taking on small fry. Husband Matt had died two years earlier, at age forty-two, and she'd married miner Anton Klemencic. And they had acquired, or would soon acquire, a boardinghouse, which had been Bara's goal ever since her stay in Klein. She never had any children with Anton.

It's revealing that less than a decade later she happily had Merlin's daughter Mary and Luka's daughter Lara come live with her and Anton in the boardinghouse. Bara didn't do favors unless there was something in it for her. With Lara and Mary, there was: free labor! For there was much work to do in this dingy flophouse that featured a sleazy bar and restaurant on the ground floor. And as for the clientele, Danis Vidmar will soon weigh in on that. It's not clear how Bara treated Mary, who remained with her for many years. But Bara worked Lara like a slave. Lara had to put in time before heading to school, on hands and knees scrubbing the barroom's filthy floor. And in the evening she toiled hours more.

Lara's hatred of Bara reached a fever pitch one evening as they stood in the kitchen arguing after Bara refused to let her go out with a friend. Feisty Lara grabbed a pan of sizzling potatoes and flung the contents at Bara, who in turn gave her a savage thrashing. Bara took her to the train station and purchased a one-way ticket back to Roundup.

■ ■ ■

At age twenty, Danis Vidmar accepted a ride with a friend who was driving to the East Coast, figuring he could visit Aunt Bara, whom he didn't remember at all, since he was less than two years old when she left Roundup for good. What follows is Danis's own account:

I didn't take too well to Aunt Bara, who was the bossiest woman I ever met. She tried hard to talk me into living there, and finding a job. But I hated the place. I couldn't take being locked up in a bar like that, with people drinking and dancing all night. I couldn't sleep because of the noise.

One of the two cleaning ladies lived in the hotel, and at night she'd pick up men at the bar and take them to her room. She was married, and had a baby, but was separated from her husband. The husband would drop by from work in the afternoon, and take the little boy to his place for the night. That made it real easy for the wife, who did this night after night. She even got fresh with me a few times. I could see why my sister Lara hated her aunt and the hotel, especially after living for so long in a strict Catholic orphanage. The hotel was a mighty wicked place.

My aunt and uncle knew what was going on, but they didn't care. Not as long as they were selling drinks, and renting rooms. There's no way I ever would have lived there. Still, my aunt worked me over to make me change my mind. One day she took me downtown, and bought me a nice topcoat, and some other clothes.

Another reason I hated the place was that it was so darned ugly, with steel mills close by, and the sky always filled with thick black smoke.

Danis would only see Bara one more time, when he was in the Army and he and new wife Gerry were stationed in Dayton, Ohio. Eager to see Danis and meet his wife, Bara packed her bags and headed for Ohio, taking along niece Mary and Mary's young son. A photo from the visit shows mannish Bara, looking like a Mafioso in a helmet-like black hat and black trench coat. All that's missing is a tommy gun. During a stroll downtown, Bara bought Danis and Gerry wristwatches. Mary's boy marred the

get-together, Danis said, because he was an obnoxious brat. Back at the
hotel, Bara lashed the boy's fanny with a leather belt.

Danis continued:

> She tried to get me and Gerry to meet with her somewhere
> for a second visit, but I couldn't get leave, and I wrote her
> so, explaining I'd be AWOL if I did what she wanted. But
> that didn't do any good. She wrote back saying how in-
> considerate I was, and how angry she was. I wrote again,
> trying to make peace. But it was no good. She must have
> stayed mad because she never answered my letter. I never
> heard from her again.

■ ■ ■

In 1958, the Grim Reaper paid seventy-one-year-old Bara an unexpected
call in Pittsburgh, when she was riding a streetcar on her way back to
the boardinghouse in Cheswick. A few days prior she'd suffered a minor
stroke and was hospitalized. As she whiled away the hours in bed, she began to feel a growing anxiety.

Because she'd lived through the Great Depression, when banks failed
and customers lost their money, Bara kept an undetermined amount of
cash hidden in the boardinghouse. Now she feared someone would find
her treasure and steal it. She simply had to get back home. Somehow she
managed to change into her own clothes and slip out. Nobody was going
to stop Bara from doing what Bara had to do.

It's a moot point as to whether she sensed the Reaper had climbed
aboard the car, because it seems her lights went out all at once due to
an even more powerful stroke. Just like that, the car had become Bara's
hearse.

2

FRIDAY THE THIRTEENTH

Danis Vidmar talked so much about father Luka's cruelty that his own son, Lawrence, thought he was exaggerating. After all, the granddad Lawrence knew was no monster. Though crude and rude, Luka was a kindly old man who enjoyed giving his grandchildren silver dollars. There wasn't a trace of his former baby-faced-killer look. Instead, Luka had morphed into a notably handsome senior. The icy gray eyes had thawed, and the dark locks had turned snowy white, as thick as ever. Sagging jowls had tempered the large chiseled jaw, and the Cupid-bow lips had lost their youthful sneer.

Lawrence's objection prompted me to ask James Vidmar to see if he could uncover any dirt on his granddad. Surely a man so violent must have run afoul of the law. So James and wife Karen drove the fifty miles from their home in Billings to Roundup. First stop was the sheriff's department. But that turned up nothing since records didn't go back that far. The Vidmars then visited the Musselshell County Courthouse, an art-deco structure from the late 1930s.

Luckily, a female clerk was happy to root through packages of documents dating back to the county's formation in 1911. It would take time since there was no handy index file. Really, it was like hunting for a needle in a haystack. It was gracious of the clerk to undertake such a task when there might not be a needle at all. Time and again she went into the storage room to retrieve the packets.

After so many trips, when it began to look like a waste of time, a "needle" showed up. Needle is perhaps too mild a word. Hypodermic is more like it. Ania Vidmar had actually filed for divorce. It was unthinkable that such a backward young woman would do such a thing—and after only ten months of marriage.

The four-page divorce petition proved that Luka's Satanic behavior was even worse than what Danis and his siblings had witnessed. It was filed four days after Luka assaulted Ania, on Friday the thirteenth of November 1914.

The incident began in the home of a neighbor, Mrs. Frank Ososki, when Ania paid a visit with her four-month-old baby, Anton (Tony). She'd gone there while Luka was away. Suddenly he stormed into the house wielding a "large club," wrote attorney James Potts. He began beating Ania on the head and back, "inflicting painful and grievous wounds."

Ania ran outside, but Luka caught up and "whipped and beat her" on the dirt street in clear view of onlookers. He then dragged her into their own home. Once inside, Potts wrote, Luka "again assaulted Ania, beating and whipping her." When Ania screamed for help, Luka "choked and strangled her." He also called her "vile names and uttered threats against her life. He then ejected her from her home and told her if she tried to come back he would kill her."

That wasn't the first time Luka had abused Ania. Potts wrote that from the first days of their marriage Luka had treated Ania "in a cruel and inhuman manner by compelling her to perform services she was unable to perform without grievous danger to her health and life."

Potts left out a significant detail: Ania was pregnant for six of those ten months, so there was a danger for the fetus, too.

The attorney went on to write that Luka on a regular basis "has struck, beaten, and bruised plaintiff and whipped her, and called her vile and opprobrious names."

Potts doesn't bring up the reason for Luka's savage attack at the neighbor's house, nor does he mention the work that endangered her health. But it's easy to figure out.

Since the coal camp shacks lacked plumbing, simply procuring water was a major task. It had to be pumped by hand from a communal well. One can be certain that it was beneath lazy Luka's dignity to stand in line at the well and pump pail after pail of water. The Vidmars used a small metal tub for bathing, and one can imagine Ania, heavy with child, struggling to haul such a weighty load from the well to the house.

The Vidmar brothers were also involved in making and selling beer. Merlin made it, and Luka sold it at his home. It's possible Ania was involved in transporting it. She also had to wait on patrons who dropped by.

It was widely known that Luka treated his bride as little more than a beast of burden, which, along with sex, was all he wanted from her. The hallmark of a psychopath is a lack of conscience. That was Luka, all right, unable to stand in others' shoes and feel their pain.

It's all but certain that the reason he attacked Ania at the neighbor's house was because he'd forbidden her to waste time socializing when there was always work to be done. He also suffered from OCD (obsessive-compulsive disorder) and expected his home to be spotless at all times. Danis remembered how Luka would go berserk if he saw dirt that others had tracked into the house. And he demanded total order. As the family grew, Ania was incapable of keeping the kind of clean and tidy home Luka demanded.

Danis never forgot Luka's OCD meltdown when he spotted a hair in a big platter of breakfast omelet Ania had just placed on the table. He cursed and screamed, hurled the platter to the floor, and stormed out of the house.

Since the attack at Mrs. Ososki's, Potts wrote, Ania "has been compelled to live among friends and neighbors, and has been supported by charity by said neighbors … plaintiff is the mother of a small child, four months of age, and is unable to earn a livelihood for herself and said child … defendant has been earning a monthly wage of about one hundred dollars per month, and is able to contribute to the support of said plaintiff and said minor child."

Potts proposed that Luka pay Ania fifty dollars monthly alimony as well as the one-hundred-dollar attorney fee.

Ania could never have acted alone in seeking a divorce, since that was beyond her competency level. Some angel of mercy had come to the rescue and rushed her off to the attorney. Never mind that divorce ran counter to her Catholic faith. This was a life-and-death crisis.

James and Karen were flabbergasted that something as unexpected as a divorce petition had shown up.

"No one knew about it," Karen said. "No one had ever said a thing about it."

James's reaction: "Wow! I didn't think the abuse went back that far, to the start of their marriage. I was shocked."

The courthouse clerk then handed over another document in which Potts stated that Ania had decided to drop the divorce proceedings. He didn't explain why.

"I can understand it," said Karen, "because she felt trapped. She didn't feel she could get by on her own. She had no alternative."

It stands to reason that Ania, unschooled and illiterate, experienced total panic at being responsible for the welfare of herself and her baby.

Another possibility is that Luka or Merlin, or both, bullied her into dropping the petition. Coming from a staunchly patriarchal society, they must have been outraged that childlike Ania could walk away and have Luka support her and a baby that wasn't his. Moreover, Potts was seeking half his salary to support them.

It was a sad outcome because Ania initially had wanted to be free of Luka forever. In the petition Potts noted that she "prays ... that the bonds of matrimony ... be dissolved." Moreover, since she was illiterate, Potts read the entire complaint to her, and she agreed it was all true.

That unknown angel of mercy had tried and failed.

The poor sprite was doomed.

3

A BRIEF TRIP BACK A HUNDRED MILLION YEARS

As the years rolled along, Klein became less and less the raw and rugged outpost it had been when the mine was a tent city. Eventually its denizens enjoyed houses that now had electricity and running water. But privies were there to stay.

Life in the camp would always leave much to be desired, but even after the mine shut down, a number of aging miners and their spouses stayed put. They'd developed a deep affection for the place.

James Vidmar, who grew up there, was so nostalgic he frequently drove up from his home in Billings, parked his car, and just let his mind drift back to ghosts from the past. But some of those ghosts had had no affection at all for the camp. One was a sad old hermit who lived across the street from the Vidmars. Joe Kezel, a Slovenian immigrant who'd spent decades in the mine, was slowly dying from black lung disease.

"I'd see him hacking and coughing up black phlegm and struggling to get air," James said. "He'd yell out in Slovene, 'bente boga.' I always thought he was screaming 'bent bucket.' When I asked Mom, she refused to tell me what the Slovene words meant. But I asked around and found out. The second word was God. The first word ... well, it wasn't for delicate ears. One day they found Joe Kezel hanging from a noose in his shack."

There were a number of oddballs who made a lasting impression on James, such as Cocky Orr, a short, ruddy-faced old miner who always wore a fedora. When grocery shopping, he'd move slowly down the aisles, picking up items and examining the prices.

"Many a time," said James, "he'd explode with rage. 'Sonofabitch! Price is up two cents!' He was such a cheapskate he sharpened worn-out razor blades. I also heard he used to visit prostitutes in Billings. He didn't drive—his wife took him, delivering him to the 'crib' of his choice."

Today there are few reminders of the camp that was. The Milwaukee Road removed the train tracks, and company houses were either moved away or torn down. Nothing remains of the boardinghouse, the company store, or the amusement hall. Because they were built of stone, the mine structures were left alone, and they still stand, but roofs have rotted away and collapsed. The tipple—a derrick-like iron structure that once towered over the mine shaft—lies on the ground in fragments.

The big hole was capped with a concrete slab with a small metal trapdoor at its center. A sturdy padlock keeps nosy visitors from harm's way. There's space enough to drop a pebble into the hole, and if you do so it takes a long time before you hear a ping echo eerily as it strikes the flooded bottom. It's a deep drop, 360 feet, the height of a thirty-six-story building. The mine had the distinction of being the deepest west of the Mississippi.

Workers may have thought the mine would operate forever, since there's so much coal down there, even after twenty million tons were extracted. And when they heard it would close after a forty-seven-year run, they were deeply shocked. But nothing on earth is forever. The mine's demise was just a matter of time after diesel fuel began to replace coal on the Milwaukee's trains.

The mine's brief history, from 1909 to 1956, was but a nanosecond in the planet's 4.5-billion-year existence. If we turn back the clock by one hundred million years, nearly all of Montana was at the bottom of an ocean that reached a depth of up to half a mile. It extended from the Arctic Ocean to the Gulf of Mexico and took up a wide swath of the nation's midsection. Geologists call it the Western Interior Seaway. It's hard to picture desertlike Musselshell County lying beneath such an immense body of water, where bizarre sea creatures once swam. The most terrifying was the snakelike mososaur, which could reach a length of thirty-seven feet and was equipped with double rows of huge spiked teeth, along with incisors on the roof of its mouth. Today's great white shark is a guppy next to this ferocious *T. rex* of the sea.

As the Rocky Mountains began to rise, perhaps topping off at twenty thousand feet, the sea was pushed eastward, and at one point south-central Montana was on the sea's western edge. Rivers originating in the western highlands irrigated the region, so that today's Musselshell County was once part of an immense swamp. As vegetation rotted, river silt buried it, and after eons the decayed matter was compacted into coal, and the silt into sandstone, which dominates today's rugged landscape. The proliferation of rimrocks in the Bull Mountains and elsewhere point out the sea's ancient shorelines.

The most spectacular rims can be seen in Billings, rising up to six hundred feet above the Yellowstone River Valley.

The Western Interior Seaway was actually a precursor to the Mississippi River.

The processes that have made Musselshell County what it is today are still at work, but we can't see what's going on because it's just too darned slow. A big rock formation like Steamboat Butte, just east of Roundup, looks as if it's been there forever and will remain that way forever. But it hasn't, and it won't.

Who knows—in a few hundred million years rising seas may once again flood the region. And monsters like the mososaur could once again prowl the ocean and gobble up every living thing in sight, right about where today's cowboys are grazing their herds.

4

THE SHORT, UNHAPPY LIFE OF ANIA VIDMAR

"We thought of her as one of us," said Danis Vidmar, trying to explain what his mother was like. The children saw her more as a big sister than a mother. Her childlike nature made a strong impression on Danis, who was two months shy of his sixth birthday when she died. She was just as defenseless as the children in dealing with grizzly bear Luka.

Luka meted out equal measures of violence against Ania and the older children. On the wall there hung a razor strop, which gave them the willies because Luka used it as much to thrash them as to sharpen his straight razor.

In today's world men like Luka often end up behind bars. But he got away with his criminal misdeeds with impunity, such as the horrific way he beat Ania on that terrible Friday the thirteenth. Neighbors kept quiet. Didn't want to get involved. But then, it was a different world. Today's media pounds away on the subject of abuse daily all across America, and witnesses are more prone to report it.

James Vidmar said folks in Roundup didn't care at all what was happening in the coal camps. That raises an interesting point; the violence in the divorce petition was bad enough for attorney Potts to refer the matter to the sheriff. But he apparently didn't. Had the law stepped in, it's unlikely

Ania would have ended divorce proceedings, at least so soon after the attack.

However, the county did take action against Luka after Ania's death because of his failure to properly feed and clothe the six children. The county provided the goods and docked Luka's salary. Not long after that, the sheriff personally escorted three of the children by train to an orphanage in Great Falls, and the other three ended up in foster care.

Even when Ania was alive, the family often went hungry. When food was put on the table, Danis said, no one was allowed to sit until Luka ate the lion's share, leaving little behind. The older children—Tony, Tomas, Lara, and Danis—would hang out at the mine and beg workers for lunchbox leftovers.

One reason for the hunger was because Luka put in so little time at the mine. Danis said he was always making excuses, such as having a headache or upset stomach. But everyone knew what the problem was: Luka was lazy as sin. But when Model T's began showing up more and more on the dirt roadways, Luka worked long and hard to rustle up enough cash to buy one. When he did, he totaled it as he drove it home for the first time, an event young Danis witnessed from the house. Luka lost control of the vehicle and rolled it.

■ ■ ■

Miners hated Luka so much that they came close to murdering him when he spoke up in defense of Germany after President Woodrow Wilson made a belated decision to enter World War One. Luka's arrogant praise of the enemy made miners bristle with anger. The camp's South Slavs were united in support of the war against Germany. Older miners had sons who'd enlisted in the U.S. Army. They were proud to be Americans, and they viewed Luka as a traitor.

A mob converged on Luka and began beating the tar out of him. Julia Virga said they would have killed him had stepfather Merlin not arrived on the scene with a shotgun. The *Roundup Record* reported that the sheriff jailed Luka overnight for his own protection. This incident would explain why the Vidmars packed it up and moved, first to Coal Camp No. 3, then to the coal camp at Acme, Wyoming, on the outskirts of Sheridan.

The only photo from Acme shows Ania standing in the doorway of the family shack, with daughter Lara, who was just learning to walk, standing on a small stoop. It's a depressing scene on several counts. The rundown shack is slum property. The clapboard siding could use paint, the stoop is flimsy, and the ground is without grass, just dirt with a few items of litter. Beautiful Lara, who would retain her good looks as an adult, is the only bright spot, having been dolled up in a fancy frock and pantalettes. Although she was the reason for the picture, it's Ania who draws the eye. Even though we can't make out the expression on her blurred face, we sense a listlessness about her. If she were fully engaged with the picture-taking, it would seem she'd have happily dropped to her knees alongside her little girl, who looks like an angel.

It's almost as if Ania wanted to hide from the camera, remaining in the shadow of the doorway. She's wearing a nondescript floor-length print dress and bib apron. And her belly is swollen with fifth child Danis—five pregnancies in less than seven years.

The real shock comes when one compares this picture with the two bridal photos, which show a vibrant teenager who must have felt she'd just entered wonderland. She was gowned and coiffed in ways she never could have imagined. Clearly, a fairy godmother or two had transformed the humble little chambermaid into Queen for a Day. The most likely helpers were Maria Meznarik and her sister Louise, who married Merlin six months later. That Bara Stupak isn't in the photo showing guests with the bride and groom suggests she'd already left for Pennsylvania.

Ania's stringy dark locks were trimmed and whipped into a frenzy of curls that barely peek out from beneath a floral cap. Attached to it is a long veil that frames her shoulders like gossamer wings of a sprite.

This is the photo referred to earlier, in which barrel-chested Merlin stands like a sentinel behind Luka, who's seated alongside Ania. Luka's expression is strong evidence that this affair wasn't his idea. He has a sour what-am-I-doing-here? look. It's a face fit for an Old West poster: WANTED DEAD OR ALIVE.

■ ■ ■

What lured Luka back to Klein was kin. Since he'd left, Bara Stupak and her son had begun to spend their summers in Roundup, and older brother Blaz, who'd immigrated ahead of his wife, had come to Klein for a brief stay.

But if Luka was happy to see Blaz again, those good feelings did not last long. Psychopathic Luka was subject to paranoia. He began to read meaning in the way Blaz looked at Ania, and it preyed on him. He imagined Blaz visited when he was away, presumably to enjoy Merlin's homemade beer, but with the aim of seducing Ania. So Luka ordered Ania to turn him away next time he came.

All hell broke loose when Luka returned home one day to learn that Ania had disobeyed him. Luka pumped six-year-old Tony for details of the visit. He wanted Tony to admit that his worst suspicions were true, that Blaz and Ania had engaged in intimacy. He pulled out a stick of candy from his pocket and held it up to Tony's face. "Tell me," he said, "that they touch each other, and I give you this candy."

It goes without saying that if Luka let his kids go hungry he wasn't in the habit of treating them to sweets. It didn't take much prodding for Tony to shake his head yes. Whereupon Luka proceeded to beat the daylights out of Ania.

Tony remained guilt-ridden for life over lying, and the terrible pain his mother had suffered because of it. He cared deeply about her, and when he reached adolescence he started trying to protect her from Luka's fists. He'd throw himself between the pair, knowing full well Luka would beat him up, too, or else reach for the razor strop. But he never quit trying, and there came a day when he fought back with more fury than Luka expected. It eventually led Luka to draw back.

But before that time came, he gave Tony the worst beating ever. Designated to watch his siblings when Luka and Ania left the house, Tony forgot about his dad's warning to keep the gate of their garden closed to the chickens. When the couple returned, Luka went berserk after he saw how the birds had demolished the vegetables, all because of Tony's negligence. He not only pummeled Tony with his firsts, he knocked him to the ground and kicked him mercilessly. Tony called it the worst beating he ever got.

As for Blaz Vidmar, he soon left for Pennsylvania, where he died in 1925.

■ ■ ■

As if things weren't bad enough, Ania bore two more children in the mid-1920s, a boy and a girl, bringing the total to six. Eight people in a four-room shack. Danis put it well when he said, "With each kid, Luka just got meaner and meaner." Seldom a day went by when he didn't pound them with his fists or whip them with the razor strop.

Third-born Tomas suffered the most abuse because, like his mother, he was a slow learner who didn't take direction well. And Luka wasn't bright enough to make allowances for their shortcomings. What drove him to heights of fury was that Tomas was a bed wetter. He tried to cure the boy by making him wear Lara's dresses and tying him to the kitchen table. When that failed, he made him sleep outside.

Although Ania had six children to tend to, and endless chores to work her way through, Luka forced her to return to her old job at the Klein boardinghouse, and he hired a babysitter. He did it because the boardinghouse allowed her to take home leftovers from supper each night.

Danis never forgot how tired his mother looked when she returned home, her arms filled with sacks of food. The poor woman was as much a beast of burden as donkeys that spent their entire lives pulling heavy coal cars in the bowels of the earth, animals that never saw the light of day.

■ ■ ■

September 28, 1926

It's a week into autumn, with a chill in the air. But the atmosphere in the Vidmar shack is chillier now that everyone, save Luka, is sick. Among the youngsters, faces are turning red due to measles. It's a wretched scene, with six youngsters crammed into two beds. Ania tries her best to deal with the situation, and she's in a bad state, too. But it's not measles. As she moves about, she leaves behind a trail of blood.

No one knows where Luka is.

Growing weaker by the hour, Ania curls up on the floor next to the coal stove for warmth. She beckons twelve-year-old Tony and asks him to go to the boardinghouse and tell the managers she can't report for work. Tony leaves, and seven-year-old Lara plants herself at her mother's side. She'll always remember Ania weeping and saying, "Baby, I going to die." A heavy thing to tell a child, but then, Ania is still a child herself.

■ ■ ■

A car pulls up, doors slam, and the voices of two women can be heard, those of Emelia Cerise, the latest wife-manager, and a woman who has been the family babysitter.

Emelia at thirty-five is an energetic, take-charge type who knows from what Tony said that the situation is dire. Right away she drove to the baby-sitter's house so that she can watch the children if Emelia has to take Ania to the hospital.

In a crisis, however, Emelia tends to panic initially before she stands ramrod straight and takes action. So she first shrieks with horror when she sees the state of affairs in the home, and is outraged that Luka is playing hooky at a time like this. It breaks her heart to see her poor little worker curled up on the floor in a blood-soaked blanket. Emelia can see she has to rush Ania to the Roundup hospital at once. And, from the looks of it, it may be the last the children ever see of her.

She and the woman lead the older children to Ania's side to say good-bye, explaining she has to leave them for a time. They kiss her, and the women take her away. The children are all in tears as they watch their mother carried out like a sack of potatoes.

■ ■ ■

Tony is the only one who is old enough and has seen enough to know what has happened to Ania. The previous day a strange woman came to the house, and she and Ania went into the bedroom and shut the door. Soon there was a commotion within, and curiosity got the better of Tony. Opening the door, he saw Ania writhing on the bed, a bed full of blood, with the strange woman in a panic, trying to prevent Ania from moving. For Tony, what was even more frightening was a blood-soaked fleshy object on the floor.

When the woman spotted Tony she hissed, waving him away as she shoved the object under the bed. As Tony shut the door in shock, he was shutting the door on his childhood. What he'd just witnessed was the aftermath of an abortion (a boy), which the midwife had botched, having punctured Ania's uterus with a knitting needle.

■ ■ ■

Ania languished three days in the hospital before drawing her last breath. The *Roundup Record*, which expressed shock at Ania's demise, reported that the funeral procession to the graveyard two miles away was one of the largest ever witnessed.

Conspicuously absent during Ania's last hours was her husband. He'd never visited her in the hospital, and when she was pronounced dead, no one knew where to find him. How could he have vanished after such a traumatic event? The abortion had been his idea, and it was he who had picked out the midwife. He must have seen that Ania was bleeding. And what about the children? How could he abandon them when they were all suffering from measles? Was he afraid the law would come after him? Or did he want to be forever free of Ania?

■ ■ ■

In later life Tony would regale his son with accounts of the coal camp's more outrageous characters. One of them was Frank Shiffler, a lanky miner who sported a Mountie-style hat and thick mustache and drove a tin lizzie. Old Frank didn't have much regard for the human race. Whenever he condemned the actions of malefactors, he'd bellow in a deep wooly voice: "They shoulda shot him before he was born!"

That's surely what he would have said about Luka Vidmar, the most hated man in Musselshell County.

■ ■ ■

Since Luka had no desire to marry again, the children would have to be put up for adoption, but it didn't happen all at once. He continued to hire the same sitter, but the children were so neglected that the county, as noted earlier, stepped in to provide food and clothing. When Luka refused to cover the costs, the county sued to have the money deducted from his wages.

After about a year, the six children were removed to foster care, but with less than desirable results. The two youngest, Mark, age four, and Ann, age two, fared best. A farm family in the Billings area took in Mark, and though he was properly cared for, the husband and wife were harsh taskmasters who caused him much grief. The husband was a judge who had lofty scholastic expectations that Mark was unable to meet. Tony and Tomas stayed with the couple briefly. But Tony rebelled against the harsh treatment and was removed. And the couple had Tomas taken away because he was a slow learner and a bed wetter.

■ ■ ■

Meanwhile, a Klein mine electrician was on the lookout for someone to stay with his widowed mother, who lived alone on her homestead, midway between Roundup and Billings. Zalka Brodar at fifty-six was in a precarious situation, completely out of touch with the outside world. There was no electricity, no radio, no telephone, no motorized vehicle. In an emergency Zalka would be helpless. She had a wagon and a few horses that her late husband had raised, but she'd never learned to handle a horse and wagon. Life on this godforsaken acreage, in the middle of nowhere, was little different from that of pioneers going way back.

Zalka's son Stan accepted Luka Vidmar's offer to let him take Danis and Lara for the summer, when school was out. The children were then staying with Merlin, second wife Lucy, and their three youngsters. It was a reckless move since the children would also be at risk in an emergency. All it would take was a snakebite in a region crawling with rattlers.

It was soon decided that when the children returned to Roundup, Tony would join Zalka. At age thirteen, he was old enough to provide the kind of help Zalka needed. The boy's time with Zalka would alter his life—and that of Zalka's—in ways neither could have expected.

5

LONG ROAD TO A DEAD END

Martin and Zalka Brodar, of Slovenia, began their New World odyssey in a coal camp at Fort Smith, Arkansas. She was three months pregnant when they exchanged vows during their first year there, on December 31, 1904. He was thirty-six, she thirty-three.

Martin was a notorious hothead who left behind a long trail of enemies. Zalka said her parents had pleaded with her to leave him. She made light of it, saying in her broken English, "I no geeve him up, he be too good-lookin'." She said her folks feared he would harm her, which suggests Martin had abused her.

His temper was scary. On one occasion he accused her of being unfaithful because she'd been too chummy with a traveling salesman. He grabbed an ax and chopped to ribbons the stockings she'd bought.

There are no other anecdotes about Martin's temper tantrums. He died before any grandchildren came along, and his children didn't tell their children much about him. Zalka grieved long and hard after his passing, but she didn't talk much about him, either.

The full scope of his bad nature can be deduced from first-born son Stan. (Stan was the mine electrician who, in the last chapter, arranged for Luka Vidmar's children to stay at the homestead with Zalka.) Stan was said to have been a chip off the old block. If so, the following anecdotes provide an idea of what his old man was like.

Stan once chased his wife with an ax after she ran his Model T into a creek.

Stan ordered a boy who was helping Zalka one summer to capture a huge rat with his bare hands. "Don't let go!" he shouted. "It'll bite you if you do!" He then grabbed a shovel and pummeled the animal to death as the terrified boy tightly held onto the tail.

After a hailstorm ruined homestead crops, the boy watched in amazement as Stan carried on as if Armageddon had arrived. He yelled and screamed to the high heavens then fell to his knees and bawled like a baby.

The boy saw Stan pull out a rifle on a "friend" during a fiery argument and threaten to kill him.

Stan's son said, "You didn't want to live next door to him."

After Arkansas the Brodars migrated to Montana, where Martin worked for a time in a coal camp near Bozeman. Next stop was a mine at Red Lodge, where he threw aside his pickax and started up a meat market in this exceedingly picturesque town at the foot of the Beartooth Mountains. The business, however, failed because, according to Zalka, Martin allowed customers to run up charges they never settled. Well, that was Zalka's spin. It's difficult to believe this paranoid individual was quite that trusting of his customers.

This had to be a most bitter experience since Martin was slipping into middle age with nothing to show for all the years he'd struggled to make something of himself. Moreover, two more children had come along, Albin and Vivian.

The Brodars moved northeast to Roundup, where Martin went to work in Mine No. 1, two miles east of town. Mining was a stopgap measure; his plan was to build up savings that would allow him to farm on the windswept plains, which had become all the rage since Congressional passage of the Enlarged Homestead Act of 1909.

On March 6, 1911, Martin filed the first in a series of claims on a remote spot midway between Roundup and Billings. The closest settlement was three miles off, a former stagecoach stop known as Thirty Mile. Martin would never own any motorized vehicles, so travel to Billings or Roundup for supplies entailed a butt-busting twenty-five-mile trip by horse and wagon. He may have selected the location because most farmers in the area were South Slavs.

The area is mostly flat terrain accented by sandstone outcrops, the most spectacular being Steamboat Butte, which looks like a transplant from Monument Valley, Utah. Martin was among the many settlers who carved their names in the big red rock, which served as a place for family outings. It looks so ancient one would think it had been the stomping grounds for dinosaurs, too. But those critters had gone extinct long before wind, rain, and ice had sculpted the butte.

In just three months Martin built a fourteen-by-forty-foot cabin composed of squared-off logs joined with a mortar made of cement and pig hair. The gable roof was made of wood shakes. The floor plan was simplicity itself: a kitchen and bedroom separated by a wide hallway, with doors front and back. The passage thus served as a breezeway on sizzling summer days. Not that one wanted to keep those doors open too often because they might entice rattlesnakes to enter, and the area was crawling with them. The living accommodations were odd inasmuch as there was only one bedroom for a family of five. But once the children reached a certain age the Brodars housed them in another structure a distance from the cabin. It's as if Martin had planned it this way, wanting the log cabin all to himself and Zalka. One evening, Viv found a rattler in her bed.

The following year he cultivated twelve acres of wheat, oats, corn, and truck gardens. That he accomplished this by himself—the children were too young to be of any help—points to an individual with Herculean staying power. His harvest in 1912 amounted to thirty-two bushels of wheat, thirty of oats, and ten of corn. Over the next three years cultivation rose to forty acres, with additional crops such as potatoes, beans, barley, and millet. In 1914 he harvested a hundred and forty bushels of corn, seventy-five of barley, and seventy of wheat.

On March 19, 1913, he became a U.S. citizen.

All those years of hard work were finally paying off. The work was brutal, but Martin was his own boss. He didn't envision his two boys carrying on as farmers, so he sent them off to board and study at a vocational school in Billings. Albin must have been thrilled by the decision, since he'd never adapted to farm life. He would always say he hated not only the homestead but all of Montana. Early on he dreamed of acquiring skills that would allow him to find work in an Eastern metropolis. Stan was never too keen on the homestead, either, but he lacked Albin's imagination. With the boys away, Viv, the youngest, must have led a lonely existence, since there were no other children living nearby. She was too smart not to grasp that because she was female she wasn't entitled to the same privileges as her brothers. As we will see later, it seems the homestead years may have had an adverse effect on her emotionally.

For seven years the Brodars and other farmers throughout eastern Montana enjoyed better-than-average rainfall. The first hint of trouble started in the spring of 1916 in the state's northeastern corner. April skies should have been gray, but the blazing sun crashed the party. Then farmers witnessed clouds of surpassing ugliness as great armies of locusts swooped in from the horizon, devouring the drought-stricken crops. Then cutworms and wireworms wriggled their way into the blighted fields to finish the job. When spring gave way to the scorching heat of summer, runaway grass fires blackened the land.

The next year drought spread throughout the eastern half of the state, with summer temperatures soaring to 110 degrees. Ferocious windstorms blew cultivated fields clear up to the sky. And the dusters would persist because farmers had cut down all that "useless" buffalo grass that had held the thin topsoil in place for many millennia. Humans had unwittingly caused far more damage than any plague of locusts.

Just like that, the Treasure State's pioneer era came to a grinding halt. Homesteaders were forced to flee or face starvation. And flee they did. It turned into a mass exodus, with between sixty thousand and seventy thousand people leaving the state for good, making Montana the only state in the union to lose population during the 1920s. Banks and businesses failed, and scores of communities that owed their birth to the homestead boom became ghost towns overnight. The state itself was plunged into economic chaos years before the Great Depression swept the nation. And when it did, Montanans were so badly battered and bruised they hardly blinked.

■ ■ ■

It was the worst nightmare Martin Brodar had ever faced. He'd poured his life's savings into the endeavor, and what earnings he'd reaped had been plowed back into the operation. He now faced ruin, and starting over from scratch wasn't a happy prospect for a man in his fifties. He forged ahead with an idea few farmers would have entertained more than five minutes. Since there was coal on the property, he'd become a coal-mine operator.

Of course, it wasn't as easy as swinging a pickax and piling the bitumen onto a wagon to sell to the few farmers who hadn't yet pulled up stakes. Being a homesteader entailed following numerous government regulations for a specified period of time before the farmer owned the land outright. Nor could the farmer start digging up any mineral deposits without getting permission. On September 21, 1921, Martin applied to the General Land Office for a mining permit on one section of his land.

The U.S. Geological Survey gave initial approval, but there were strings attached. Martin would have to pay a fifteen-cent royalty on each ton of coal, invest at least $500 in the operation for three years, and be required by year four to mine 285 tons of coal. But it was up to the land office to decide, and that meant lots of red tape. It took thirteen months before Martin got the green light.

Because of his mining experience, Martin understood the nuts and bolts involved in the work at hand. It was a huge undertaking, especially since he didn't have any motorized vehicles. Just acquiring the needed materials from either Billings or Roundup and transporting them was a huge undertaking. But now his sons were in their late teens. With their vocational-school backgrounds, they could have left the fold. But they didn't, possibly because of the hold their domineering father had on them. Martin put them to work, as he did any number of South Slavs in the neighborhood; whenever he filed applications, these workers signed as witnesses. In time, however, those ethnic members were replaced by Anglo-Saxon names in later applications. A neighbor of the Brodars, a youngster at the time, would explain the reason decades later: Martin was a ruthless boss who alienated those men, causing them to quit.

When the coal seam played out, Martin didn't bother filing more applications for other sections on his land—not when he might have to wait another year for approval. He simply began ripping into various hillocks. He knew it was unlikely any government official would visit to make sure he complied with the law. In later life son Stan crowed: "Boy-oh-boy! I remember when folks came here and bought a hundred and sixty dollars worth of coal in one day!"

Martin had thus managed to survive the horrors of drought and periodic insect invasions. But little did he know that time was running out on him, at age fifty-six. He got involved in a dispute with another homesteader over a road right of way. It appears the other party tried to prevent him from using the road. It must have turned into a major brouhaha because Martin decided to bring the matter before Yellowstone County commissioners. This was a major undertaking, since it meant that twenty-five-mile butt-busting trip by horse and wagon over rough dirt roadways. There are no details on the outcome of that mission.

Albin drove the wagon on the way back while Martin tried to quell his anger and frustration with a bottle of booze. As they approached the homestead, Albin stopped to pick up a young neighbor. Stan sat at Albin's side while Martin and the rider stood together on one side of the wagon box. As Albin made a turn, the horses lurched forward, causing the unbalanced wagon to tip sharply to one side. The men in back were thrown to the ground. The young man was unhurt, but Martin was fatally injured.

The *Roundup Record* reported that Yellowstone County Sheriff Russell Sage ruled out foul play. Martin fell backward and "died instantly either from breaking his neck or from heart failure." Zalka said she cried every day for a year. Grief may have triggered a nervous breakdown because for ten years she didn't set foot beyond the homestead gate. And when she did it was because of advanced gum disease that required having all her teeth pulled. She remained alone on the homestead even after her children left. Albin moved to Great Falls, Stan soon got the electrician job in Klein, and Viv did the same work Ania Vidmar had done in the Klein boardinghouse. Stan and Viv spent their weekends with their mother.

■ ■ ■

It was three years after Martin's death when Danis and Lara Vidmar spent the summer of 1927 with Zalka, who housed them not in her log cabin but in the one-room abode that had served as her own children's sleeping quarters. Danis's most vivid memory was the morning he and Lara awoke with the rising sun only to find a rattlesnake slithering about. Because of the summer heat they'd left the door open. With the rattler blocking the entrance, all they could think to do was remain in bed and scream for Mrs. Brodar, whose cabin was beyond shouting distance. They just had to wait until the snake got bored and slithered back out. There were rattlers everywhere. One day, as they opened the root-cellar door, a rattler sent them fleeing in horror. They told Zalka, who killed the snake with a hoe.

No sooner had the children been returned to Klein, to board with their uncle and his family, than Tony was transferred to the homestead.

Tony never talked much about life with Zalka except to say that she had a nasty habit of preparing soup made with spoiled chicken meat. He never said whether she partook of the soup. He complained, but she ignored him. He turned to hunting rabbits. For the rest of his life he had trouble eating chicken, since it always brought back those foul memories.

Danis said Zalka was sweet to him and Lara, but she was tough as leather with others. When provoked she was like an angry rattler. She never displayed any tender loving care for Tony. From time to time he'd boast that someday soon he'd pick up and leave, make something of himself. She didn't offer an ounce of sympathy for the orphan, once jeering, "Oh yah, Tony Vidmar be big man! Where you go? What you do? Hah!" She was indifferent to his wants and needs. Each day he had to walk three miles to the schoolhouse in Thirty Mile wearing ordinary street shoes across rugged terrain, in rain and snow. One day his teacher sent him back with a note saying Zalka needed to get him overshoes. Zalka couldn't read.

Tony wasn't happy. Zalka never displayed any warmth to him, and he never felt the least affection for her. But he admired her strength—said she had a cast-iron stomach and never complained about aches or pains. Also, her cabin was so squeaky clean you could eat off the floor. What gnawed at him was that she wasn't paying him for all his hard work. Well, she didn't handle the purse strings. Stan did, and he was a tyrant. Tony complained to Stan, but it did no good. He was their captive.

After a couple of years, Tony saw a way out. His brothers Tomas and Danis had been sent to live with a Slovenian homesteader after spending time in an orphanage in Great Falls. He had no idea whether homesteader Joe Bartol would take him in. But rather than discuss the matter with his dad, whom he seldom saw, he decided to take matters into his own hands. One day he told Zalka he was leaving. She said nothing as he packed his few things and started out on foot to the Billings-Roundup highway to hitch a ride to his father's place in Coal Camp No. 3.

Neither Tony nor Zalka could have imagined they'd see one another again. How wrong they were.

6

FROM DROUGHT TO DEMENTIA

There was another local homesteader whose survivalist bent paralleled that of Martin Brodar's. He too was a loner, and a hothead, with a wide streak of paranoia. Just as Brodar had opted to farm on elevated land to monitor trespassers, Dunn also homesteaded atop a lofty ridge in the Bull Mountains. From the Brodar homestead that ridge dominates the northern horizon, being several miles long and looking like a mesa from below. Dunn's paranoia was underscored by the presence of a watchtower from which he, armed with a rifle, would look for trespassers.

Dunn was another character History was wont to forget when the tombstone went up. But in 1930 he was the talk of Roundup after killing his son-in-law. Stories of the gruesome slaying and the way lawmen got Dunn to confess were plastered all over the *Roundup Record*. Today the name William Dunn no longer means anything to locals, but the ridge where he lived is known in hiking circles as Dunn Mountain.

The *Roundup Record* said Dunn had once worked as a private investigator in Illinois. There was no information about his wife or the number of children they had. Only daughter Bessie, the victim's wife, is mentioned in the news accounts. Nor is it known when Dunn came to Montana and began homesteading. Seems he'd never had any run-ins with the law prior to the murder. But his description of his son-in-law and the events that led to the slaying are scary because they provide a peek into a deeply disturbed individual who seems to have lost contact with reality. Dunn first tried to make lawmen believe the victim had bashed his head in a fall from the roof of his own home. When that didn't wash, he said he'd killed John Harrison in self-defense. But Dunn had gone out of his way to provoke the man, who was totally soused. If he threatened Dunn with a knife, as Dunn alleged, it may have been in self-defense.

It seems reasonable to suggest that the great drought and hard times of the 1920s had further undermined Dunn's already precarious mental state. When the victim entered the life of paranoid Dunn, he pushed the homesteader over the edge. Harrison and Dunn, then, could be viewed as two casualties of the homestead fiasco.

Dunn drew lots of stares whenever he came to town with two daughters locked in a chicken-wire cage in the wagon box. He was paranoid about their safety. Afraid of wolves: the two-legged type. His downfall began one day in 1928. As he and his daughters were repairing a fence, two strangers drove up in a motorcar. One was future son-in-law John Harrison, accompanied by a man he identified as a friend and a gambler. Harrison was on a mission—to meet elder daughter Bessie. He told the Dunns he and his friend had tried to drive up to the homestead on a couple of previous occasions, but their vehicle had gotten stuck in mud.

Dunn told lawmen he took such a liking to the man he invited him and his friend to stay for supper. Perhaps he was just putting up a good front since it was apparent that Bessie was smitten with Harrison. There must have been tension in the Dunn household as John and Bessie began to see more of one another. Dunn probably would have objected to any suitor, but Harrison had two big strikes: he was not only old enough to be Bessie's dad, he was also a heavy drinker. Within weeks John and Bessie exchanged vows before a justice of the peace in Billings. He was fifty-three, she thirty-six. They settled on a nearby farm.

During grilling by lawmen, Dunn perhaps did more than a little fibbing when he talked about the good relationship he'd had with John Harrison. He said he'd frequently visited the couple in the evening and stayed the night, not caring to maneuver his wagon up steep slopes to his farm in the dark. Dunn must have witnessed numerous occasions when Harrison was drunk. Harrison wasn't behaving like a responsible husband, and Bessie was deeply unhappy. The men must have locked horns. While Harrison nursed terrible hangovers by dawn's early light, Dunn must have nursed a toxic hatred.

On January 25, 1930, Dunn paid an early visit because Bessie was bedridden with an undisclosed illness. Soon Harrison left for Roundup for medicine. But when he returned he was roaring drunk, having spent the medicine money on moonshine. As Harrison swilled booze, a yelling match ensued. When it came to murderous hatred, Dunn had met his match, and he feared Harrison might well do him harm. After their war of words, Harrison began work on a rooftop radio antenna.

Dunn stayed at Bessie's bedside. As he sat there stewing, he gazed at a vanity mirror, which reflected a gun hanging on a hallway wall. It made Dunn nervous, considering the state Harrison was in. So he fetched the pistol, removed the bullets, and put it back. He then found a hammer small enough to fit into a back pocket. Bessie suggested the best way to handle the situation was to hide the booze. Dunn snapped at her: "Don't ever take a drinking man's whiskey! He'll kill ya!"

Dunn was still at Bessie's bedside when Harrison reentered and came to the bedroom door. There must have been another yelling match because Harrison walked over to fetch the gun, unaware Dunn was watching him in the mirror. Dunn told lawmen, "I asked him if he was taking the gun to hunt moonshine."

Harrison threw the empty gun to the floor, rushed to the kitchen, and returned with a butcher knife.

"He looked like a damned demon to me!" Dunn declared. "And he shouted, 'I will kill all of ya!'" Dunn pulled out the hammer from his pocket. "I swung and hit that butcher knife and knocked it to the floor."

As Harrison bent down for the knife, Dunn screamed: "What's the matter with you? Gone crazy?" He then struck Harrison in the head with the hammer. The victim sprang to his feet and fled from the house with Dunn at his heels. "I popped him on the head again. And he run around and fell. I fancy that hard ball went through his skull. I must have hit him four times."

Dunn then fetched rope and tied Harrison's hands. He returned to Bessie's side and said, "I'm afraid John got pretty badly hurt, Bess." He said she responded, "He was up on the house, I guess he fell off the house." Dunn went outside, found a rock, and inflicted more damage to the skull. He'd make lawmen think what Bess suggested: that Harrison had fallen from the roof and smashed his head on a rock.

That underscored Dunn's dementia. Harrison looked as if he'd fallen not from a roof but from the rim of the Grand Canyon. An attorney for the county was appalled when he viewed the corpse. He told the *Billings Gazette:* "It's the most brutal slaying in the history of Musselshell County."

Lawmen grilled Dunn for hours before he broke down and confessed. After pleading guilty to second-degree murder, he was sentenced to life at hard labor in the state prison at Deer Lodge. He was sixty-three. Five years later he was transferred to the state mental hospital at Warm Springs, where he died in 1936.

7

FROM HELL TO BREAKFAST

Joe Bartol was a bigger-than-life dynamo, with the goals and energy of a dozen men. He walked tall, talked big, and sang with a voice that could fill an opera house. That's because he'd actually sung in opera houses in Italy, next door to his native Slovenia. So how on earth did an opera singer end up halfway around the world to become a Montana homesteader? That's a secret Bartol took to the grave. The fact that he still held on to his humble spread, northwest of Roundup in the Judith Basin, proves how tough he was.

He still made ends meet following the catastrophic drought that sent tens of thousands of farm folks fleeing the state forever. Bartol was involved in most everything under the sun: livestock, grain, produce, coal mining, and moonshine. Never exactly flush with cash, he sometimes borrowed money from hired help.

But Bartol had an Achilles' heel he never talked about, refusing to deal with mortality when he was only fifty years old. If he ever told anyone what ailed him, no one would remember the name. Only that it involved his lungs. Bartol was like a big balloon that each year lost a little air. By age fifty-nine the balloon went limp.

Bartol made for an amusing sight as he went about his daily duties singing arias to pigs, chickens, and cows. He surely didn't look like a homesteader. In the 1920s brother Anton snapped a photo of him seated at the wheel of his snazzy Graham-Paige roadster. You'd think he'd led a country life of leisure, donning a driving coat, ivy cap, and a big cheesy smile on his handsome face. Crouched on the roadster's running board is a tense-looking mutt.

Also in the picture are two orphaned sisters who, by contrast, could be poverty poster girls. Joe had taken them on with only one aim in mind: cheap labor. They were just old enough to be helpful. But their sloppy dress and unkempt hair suggest he didn't much care about them. It's said the girls were removed by court order. But no one knew why, and Joe never talked about it.

■ ■ ■

Joe Bartol was all ears when a moonshine customer from Roundup told him he could acquire helping hands if he was willing to serve as foster father for two boys in a Great Falls orphanage.

Shorty Remec had worked at the same mine as Luka Vidmar, and before Ania's death he'd often dropped by their house to partake of Merlin's homemade beer, which Ania served to customers. It was there that he got to know the children and developed a strong affection for one in particular, Danis.

His interest in Danis started two years back, when the boy was five. After swilling too much brew, Shorty staggered out to his black sedan, fired up the engine, shifted into reverse, and hit the accelerator, totally oblivious that the children were all around playing hide and seek. The car lurched backward, followed by screams and what Shorty perceived as a bump in the car's rear end.

Shorty may have peed his pants when he got out and saw he'd just rolled over little Danis. He and Ania were in a panic as they carried the weeping boy into the house. Although the wheels had run over Danis's legs, there was no apparent damage.

Shorty was a major menace behind the wheel. He did the greatest damage to his own property—the garage. He was the laughingstock of the coal camp because he demolished the garage wall time and again by failing to put the car into reverse. Boys in the neighborhood rebuilt it each time, then found the perfect solution: they replaced the wall with a set of doors that could be left open.

Because he'd come within inches of killing Danis, Shorty went out of his way to be nice to the boy whenever he dropped by to enjoy a few beers (always warm since the Vidmars didn't have an ice box).

"He never got over it," Danis remembered after eight decades. "He'd always sit me on his lap and feed me candy."

Joe Bartol was elated after driving out to St. Joseph's Catholic Orphanage with Luka and Shorty to meet the boys. He took a shine to Danis, who was both handsome and bright. He was less keen on taciturn Tomas.

For Danis, switching from orphanage to homestead was like going to heaven. "At last! I wasn't fenced in anymore," Danis said. "The farm looked so beautiful the first morning I was there. There was a creek with a small dam, and a white horse out in the pasture."

Although Joe Bartol had never married (same for his brother who lived nearby), he may have felt a deep-seated desire to be a daddy. He offered to adopt the boys, but Luka was unwilling to sign away rights. So Joe became their legal guardian, which Danis never knew until after Bartol's death. He insisted the boys call him daddy, but they never did so. Danis said it didn't seem right since Luka was daddy.

The boys were awed by how sweet Bartol was early on. He took them to Sunday services at the Catholic church in Lehigh, then treated them to tasty meals at a restaurant. He bought them a tepee, but on their first night in it they were forced back to the house by a violent thunderstorm that destroyed the tent. And he took them to a Christmas pageant on a horse-drawn sled, an event that gave him a bad chest cold that landed him in bed.

When the boys weren't in school they had mostly light duties, such as milking six cows each and feeding the chickens and calves. Danis had to lead the cows out to pasture in the morning before school and round them up in the evening. The boys took turns operating the cream separator at a time when cream was fetching good prices. "Old Joe," Danis said, "would take five gallons of cream to town every other day."

Bartol also taught the boys how to make moonshine, with Danis in charge. Because this was during Prohibition, Bartol lectured them time and again not to utter a word to anyone. Whenever he drove around to peddle his spirits he always took Danis along; he figured that with a kid at his side no federal agent on the lookout would suspect him of transporting contraband.

Bartol's sweet daddy act soon began to fray. He stopped bringing them to church and taking them out to eat. He loaded them with more and more work and became an exacting taskmaster. When their work didn't meet expectations, he'd lose his temper. His impatience grew by leaps and bounds, and angry words gave way to yelling and screaming. Then came the physical assaults, spankings and whippings. He'd even hurl them to the ground and kick them mercilessly.

"Sweet daddy" had morphed into another Luka. As one of the younger children, Danis hadn't suffered Luka's abuse as had the older children, Tomas in particular. Bartol's early good treatment had lifted Tomas's spirits greatly, and now the sudden cruelty took a heavy toll on him. He would live for years in a depressed state. Bartol didn't conceal how much he despised the dull, backward bed wetter, and he loaded him with backbreaking chores. Danis experienced much heartbreak for his brother.

"If Tomas did the work wrong and made Old Joe mad," Danis explained, "I'd step up and take the blame. I knew how to make Old Joe calm down, something Tomas never could do. He didn't know how to defend himself by making up some excuse."

But Tomas developed a grudge against Danis because Bartol favored his little brother—a grudge that lasted for life.

"Old Joe never wanted to be around Tomas," Danis said. "Whenever he went out for a drive he'd take me along, never Tomas."

■ ■ ■

A couple who did business with Bartol—such as trading chickens and pigs—took such a liking to Danis they got Joe's permission to have the boy stay with them a couple of weeks. On one occasion, when Danis removed his shirt, the wife was aghast at all the black and blue marks.

The couple chewed over the matter for some time, feeling they had to do something, but what? They didn't want to confront Bartol, nor did they want to report him to authorities. But being unable to keep quiet, they spread the word about Bartol's treachery. The gossip got back to Bartol, who drove to the couple's home, told them to go to hell, and dragged Danis to the car, forbidding him from ever seeing those people again. But Danis from time to time sneaked away to visit. Before long they left the area, having urged him to see the sheriff or county attorney. That was a tall order for one so young.

■ ■ ■

Danis's spirits soared when Bartol announced that Tony would soon join them. He believed that big brother wouldn't allow Old Joe to beat up on him and Tomas. He hadn't forgotten the way Tony, despite his small stature, had used his fists against Luka whenever he pounced on Ania.

Bartol wanted Tony so bad he drove the several hours it took to reach Roundup on dirt and gravel roads. Tony had been staying with Luka in Coal Camp No. 3 since leaving Zalka Brodar. At sixteen Tony had wised up to the harsh realities of life during the Great Depression, and how bad it could be on a failed homestead such as Zalka's. He didn't leap at this new offer until Bartol assured him he would feed him better than Zalka had.

Danis, who had come along with Old Joe, cringed at that bald-faced lie. Bartol had all along fed him and Tomas a substandard diet heavy on cornmeal mush. Bartol's selfishness was paramount, for he was actually a gourmet cook who whipped up tasty meals for himself and brother Anton. He even employed the boys in making hogshead cheese and garlic sausage, while never allowing them to partake of such treats.

Danis recalled: "He was the only person around who knew how to make that kind of garlic sausage, and folks loved it."

Bartol wasn't going to waste it on ranch hands when so many people were willing to pay good money for it.

Tony also wanted Bartol to promise he'd pay him wages, and Old Joe waved off his worry. Why, a young man his age deserved to be paid for his work. And again, Danis knew he was lying.

Tony, of course, was disillusioned from the start. Not only was the food lousy, but Bartol kept putting off paying him. The only thing Tony enjoyed was use of a car that had been converted into a truck. He used it to take himself and his brothers the two miles to school in Lehigh.

It was the first time Tony had ever driven a vehicle, and it gave him a sense of power and freedom. In one situation it allowed him to defy Bartol. Danis had injured his shoulder after falling from a pony, and Bartol refused to take him to a doctor. Tony took the boy aside: "C'mon, let's run like hell for the truck—before he can stop us."

Tony located a doctor in Stanford who told the boys it was a good thing they'd come to him because the shoulder would have ended up mighty crooked without treatment.

"Dr. Dismor lifted his arm, made a fist, and pounded my shoulder really hard," said Danis.

Tony passed out just watching.

"The doctor put my arm in a sling and said it would take at least six weeks to heal."

Bartol refused to lighten Danis's workload and never paid the doctor.

■ ■ ■

The boys each had a pet dog. When they returned home from school one day, a grim-faced Bartol told them the pooches had entered the pigpen and killed and injured the animals.

He then delivered the shocker: each boy would have to shoot his own pet. Tony protested strenuously, but Bartol wouldn't budge. Danis and Tomas were in tears. Tony went first, then Tomas. When it was Danis's turn he was weeping so hard Bartol took the gun away, and the dog too.

He took the dog to Lewistown and abandoned it. But the pooch found his way back, with Danis breaking into tears of joy as the dog leaped into his arms. Bartol did nothing.

■ ■ ■

"It was great having Tony around for protection," Danis said. "Whenever he caught Old Joe getting ready to clobber me or Tomas he'd hold up his fists and tell him, 'Don't you dare hit him!' He also protected us against school bullies who'd pick on me and Tomas because we were orphans. There was one kid I was afraid of, but Tony said I could beat him up if I wanted. So when that kid tried to pick a fight, I went after him, and I was winning.

"His brother, who was watching, grabbed me and threw me down into a pile of hot ashes the janitor had just dumped on the ground. Tony was there, and boy! Was he mad! He started beating up the kid—his mouth was full of blood. A teacher stuck her head out of the schoolhouse window and started yelling for Tony to stop. He yelled back that she'd better shut up or he'd beat her up too."

■ ■ ■

Bartol took away Tony's "power" by refusing to let him use the truck for school because the gas was costing too much. Tony threatened to quit school, but Bartol didn't care if any of them went to school or not. In the end, only Danis made the four-mile round trip on foot each day. Bartol pulled Tomas out because of bad grades, ostensibly, but it was really to get more work out of him.

■ ■ ■

In the months Tony was there, Bartol never fulfilled his promise of paying him wages. But Tony kept hoping, until the day came when he knew there was no hope. Bartol's nephew Paul Klobichar, who was Tony's age, came out from Minnesota to work. After the boy told Tony his uncle was paying him, Tony confronted Bartol, but it did no good. So he packed his bags, and Bartol drove him back to Roundup.

When Old Joe returned, Danis saw Tony's bags in the car. "I asked Old Joe why, and he said Tony decided he didn't want all that old stuff after all."

Danis later learned the truth. When Tony stepped out of the car at Coal Camp No. 3, Bartol hit the accelerator before Tony could get his belongings.

■ ■ ■

With Tony gone, Bartol once again slapped, punched, and kicked the boys. Matters came to a boil one day when Bartol, Danis, and a ranch hand were transporting bales of hay. Bartol drove the wagon so close to the creek bank that the wheels sank into the soil, causing the wagon to flip onto its side. No one was injured, but the horses broke free and ran off.

Bartol blasted Danis for being so stupid as to put all the bales on one side. As Danis denied it, Bartol began the old routine: slapping, punching, knocking Danis to the ground, and kicking—more viciously than ever. "Worst beating I ever got," said Danis.

Upon returning home, he packed a bag and sneaked off. His heart was in his throat because he didn't know where in hell he was headed. Just figured it was time to cut all ties with Bartol. At first he walked along train tracks in case Bartol searched for him on the highway. Then he remembered that couple's advice to report Bartol to the sheriff or county attorney.

Danis hitched a ride to Stanford, where he looked up the attorney, who heard him out, assuring him he'd take care of it.

"The next day," Danis said, "I was outside when I saw the sheriff drive up to the house. He knocked on the door, and Old Joe let him in. A while later the sheriff left. I didn't say anything to Joe about it, and he didn't, either. I'm pretty sure the sheriff told him he had to see the attorney. He never again beat me or Tomas."

■ ■ ■

One day Danis's uncle Merlin drove to the homestead with family for a visit. They'd just come from Great Falls, with Lara aboard, after taking her out of the orphanage for good. Merlin's plan was to send her to stay with her Aunt Bara, at her boardinghouse near Pittsburgh. Merlin wanted Danis to come live with them, but he refused. He didn't relish the idea of living once again in an ugly coal camp, especially in a tiny shack with Merlin and his wife and their children. Moreover, Danis knew Merlin would use him like a workhorse. And, worst of all, he didn't want to be around his uncle during one of his alcoholic binges, when he was as dangerous as a grizzly.

■ ■ ■

Bartol had given Danis a pony that gave birth to a colt the boy came to love. It was a frisky critter with white-stockinged feet and white spots on the face. Danis gave it tender loving care, and he got a horse trainer to work with it. He took great pride in riding his pony to town to show him off.

Bartol also had his eye on the colt, aware he could sell it at a good price. Many times he offered to buy it from Danis. One day, returning from school, the boy was thunderstruck that his beloved pet had disappeared. Bartol told him the animal had jumped the cattle guard and joined wild horses passing by. Though Danis felt it a fishy story, he still spent several days hunting in vain for the colt. There was no doubt Bartol had sold it.

■ ■ ■

Another example of Bartol's mean spirits involved sheep. An elderly neighbor who took a liking to Danis and Tomas gave them "bum lambs," those abandoned by their mothers. That way the boys could raise the lambs and sell them. Bartol, who'd never raised sheep, became interested. He'd visit the old man and ask if he had any bums for the boys. The rancher was always happy to oblige. But Bartol brought them to brother Anton's spread, and the pair began sheep ranching in earnest.

When Danis's and Tomas's bums matured, Bartol herded them off to Anton's place. Even after seven decades Danis couldn't talk about the lambs without bitterness.

"Tomas and I spent a lot of time caring for those lambs, hoping to sell them and get some spending money. But Old Joe never gave us one nickel for all the work we'd done."

By age thirteen, Danis couldn't stomach much more of Bartol's abuse. A showdown was inevitable.

■ ■ ■

The showdown, which took place while Luka was visiting, erupted when Bartol told Danis he could forget about entering high school. Until that day he'd been noncommittal. Furious, Danis said he'd join his dad on the bus trip back to Roundup. Bartol wouldn't budge. He didn't want to lose Danis, but he was too proud to appear weak in Luka's eyes.

With time to spare before the bus departed, Bartol dropped the pair off at a Lewistown café, gave them money for lunch, and said he'd return after running a brief errand.

Danis had no idea what sort of errand he had to run, but soon after he entered his father's house he learned that Bartol had pulled a mean trick, similar to what he'd done to Tony. The "errand" was an excuse for Bartol to park the car and rifle through his suitcase, removing items the boy cherished.

■ ■ ■

Danis had reason to think Luka had mellowed during the seven years he was in foster care. He hadn't often come up to see Danis and Tomas, but when he did he was nothing like the ogre who had once terrorized his family. Danis was now sorry he'd walked out on Bartol because Luka hadn't changed at all. Luka had allowed him to enter high school, but he expected the boy to work mighty hard for room and board. He had to do the same tedious tasks that his mother had once handled.

Like Ania, he had to draw water day and night from the communal well. That was a lot of water when one factored in what Luka would need for his bath. Danis never forgot how violent Luka became one day when he hadn't heated the water to the right temperature on the coal stove. Luka went berserk. Cursing Danis, he chased him out of the house, dragged the heavy tub to the door, emptied it, and hurled it directly at Danis.

And Danis had to take precautions never to track dirt into the house since that too could cause Luka to erupt like a volcano.

After several such episodes, Danis appealed to sister Lara and new hubby Pete Barsich to give him shelter. They agreed, but because they didn't have a second bedroom, Pete and Danis boarded up half the porch.

It was a stopgap measure at best because life there was also the pits. Lara and Pete were a hugely mismatched pair, the result of Uncle Merlin having played matchmaker, just as he had with Luka and Ania. After Bara Stupak sent Lara back to Roundup, Merlin didn't know what to do with the girl since he didn't have room in his house. So he came up with the none-too-bright idea of pairing fifteen-year-old Lara with an alcoholic miner twice her age. The man would beat her up, sending her running off in the night to stay with Luka. Life was tough enough for Danis, holed up nights in a cold, makeshift enclosure, but he also had to put up with loads of yelling and screaming from the couple. In time, however, Lara got the upper hand and learned to clobber Pete.

■ ■ ■

One afternoon, when he was down in the dumps after school let out, Danis walked aimlessly down Roundup's Main Street. It was bitterly cold, and he was hungry as a horse. Mouth-watering aromas from eateries got the best of him. Although he had only two bits to his name, he walked into Vienna Café and asked owner John Lucas if he'd serve him a quarter's worth of food. Lucas motioned him to sit at the counter next to a man awaiting his meal. Lucas brought bowls of soup for both of them. That was followed by identical plates of food.

Danis said, "I reminded John I only had a quarter, but he said nothing."

After wolfing down all that grub, Danis couldn't believe it when Lucas served pie as well. He tried to explain how he couldn't afford dessert too, but Lucas rushed back into the kitchen. At meal's end, Danis held out his quarter and said, "I'm sorry, Mr. Lucas, but this is all I have." Lucas smiled, shook a finger at him, and replied, "If that's all you have, that's all I need."

■ ■ ■

There was a ray of hope for Danis when Memorial Day rolled around. Emelia and Camille Cerise, who had been Ania Vidmar's last bosses at the Klein boardinghouse, dropped by since the missus wanted to see how Lara was doing. The Cerises had moved to a farm on the outskirts of Billings. The couple told Danis he could come work for them. When they offered fifty cents a day, he agreed. It would be the first time he ever got paid for work. He rode back with the Cerises that day.

The couple put him up in their home, but Danis soon opted to live in a train boxcar that Camille had converted into a cabin.

"Mrs. Cerise was very bossy," Danis said. "She talked all the time and picked on Camille constantly. But he never talked back. He'd just light his pipe and go about his business."

Emelia was a workaholic, with numerous irons in the fire. She planned to start up a noodle factory, which was why she wanted Danis. Right away she began training him to make pasta. Needing capital, she turned to a couple of shady characters who soon ended up getting arrested and charged with counterfeiting. So much for pasta.

■ ■ ■

Once a week Danis and two grizzled ranch hands irrigated the alfalfa crop at three in the morning. At six Emelia would serve breakfast. "One morning," Danis recalled, "Mrs. Cerise ran into the house while we were eating and started yelling that grasshoppers were invading the farm. We went outside, and sure enough, they were everywhere. They ate everything, even the paint off the fence posts. We drove to town to get banana oil to kill them, but it was too late. They left as quickly as they came."

■ ■ ■

Danis's two coworkers liked to sneak into the cellar to guzzle the Cerises' homemade beer and wine. They'd have Danis lock the door behind them so Emelia wouldn't think to look for them there. She'd go up to Danis and ask where on earth they could be. He'd just shrug and play ignorant. That wasn't the only favor he did the old boys. Over the years he'd become adept with electrical work, so he wired the cellar so the booze hounds could see what they were drinking.

■ ■ ■

The Cerises also dabbled in real estate. They bought a couple of coal-camp shacks and had them moved to the farm, a distance of forty-five miles. Their intention was to sell the houses. Tragedy struck as the second home was pulling up. Because a power line was in the way of a chimney, one of the movers climbed up to the roof; as he raised the line to clear the chimney, he was electrocuted. Danis, who saw him doubling up and falling to the ground, said, "Mrs. Cerise became hysterical. She was crying and pulling her hair out."

■ ■ ■

After a month on the farm Danis was rethreading a pipe, to be used for a well serving the houses, when a metal shard struck his eye. Luckily, it didn't do any lasting damage. The medical bill came to six dollars, which Emelia expected Danis to pay. That would mean working twelve days to cover it. Danis was so angry he walked over to a farmer down the road and was hired on the spot. His boss was an Italian who'd guzzle a pitcher of wine during long afternoon siestas. A California vintner shipped the wine to him by the barrel. He tried to entice his new ranch hand into joining him, but Danis desisted. He'd lost all interest in booze the day he and Tomas had imbibed Bartol's wine on the sly, which made him sick.

The Billings area turned out to be just as much of a bust as Roundup. Danis was stuck with a dead-end job, and he couldn't continue high school because it was too far away. He also disliked Yellowstone County's dry climate, which gave him nosebleeds. He ended up returning to the Judith Basin.

■ ■ ■

For the next three years Danis went from hell to breakfast, frantically searching but never finding good steady work with a boss willing to allow him to attend high school. For a time he herded sheep on a cold, windy mountainside, housed in a tent, calling it "the most miserable job I ever had."

The outlook was so bleak he even agreed to work briefly for Joe Bartol when his nephew had to undergo surgery. In the short time Danis had been away, Bartol's health had deteriorated markedly. He was gaunt, and crankier than ever, coughing a great deal, and he now had a housekeeper.

But Bartol never quit looking for ways to make a buck. He turned to mining coal on his land, with his brother and nephew running the show. Danis joined the team, which included a few other men. It was hard work, but it was a bust. Bartol had figured they could sell the coal in the nearby towns, but door-to-door sales were pathetic.

Danis went to work for rancher Bill Hughes during hay season, but he didn't stay long. Hughes and his wife became distraught when their horses began dying from sleeping sickness, transmitted by flies. Hughes was so torn up over this catastrophe that he had temper tantrums as bad as those of Joe Bartol. Danis and coworker Bob Marshall collected their last paychecks, with Hughes imploring them to return when things got back to normal.

Danis and Bob hopped a train boxcar for Great Falls, where they spent a few days holed up in a hobo camp. When they were about to enter a downtown eatery, a cop tried to stop them because they were so smelly and dirty. Danis said a young gal told the officer to quick picking on those poor cowpokes.

The two comrades then rode the rails to Billings, with Danis figuring they could work for his former bosses, Emelia and Camille Cerise. It was a miserably long walk from the train tracks to the farmhouse, but they got a royal welcome from the couple. Emelia begged them to stay, but they were so hard up all they could offer was room and board. The young men helped out for a few days, but they needed to earn some bucks. Sad-eyed Emelia put together some produce in a box for them to take, and Camille drove them to the bus station, where Danis gave away most of the food.

Bob Marshall felt their best bet was to check out the N Bar Ranch. The ranch, which began operating in the 1880s, was, and still is, a Montana landmark. After stepping off the bus, Danis and Bob had to walk many foot-blistering miles to reach the ranch, whose specialties at the time were Black Angus cattle and sheep. After all that trekking, and with their hopes so high, Danis and Bob were in despair to learn there were no openings. Ranch hands, however, urged them to enquire at two nearby sawmills.

The young men were elated as they both found jobs at the mills. They then built themselves a one-room hut alongside a creek. They even made their own furniture: bunk beds, table, and two chairs. And they bought a wood stove. Each earned a buck fifty a day.

They pooled their money and bought an old jalopy. By midwinter, the car needed engine work, so they drove to a shop in Lewistown where Bartol had his vehicles serviced. Danis struck up a conversation with the owner, who extended his condolence over Bartol's death. No one had told Danis Old Joe had died.

The news hit Danis so hard he insisted they drive right away to Bartol's place. It was a wretched seventy-mile trip on icy roadways. They had to make emergency stops at farmhouses, begging for hot water to thaw out the frozen radiator. Even after seventy years Danis could remember how his frozen hands throbbed with pain.

The sight of Bartol's last in a series of homes—a two-story red farm-house—was a huge relief for the tired and hungry travelers. But Bartol's brother and nephew gave them the cold shoulder. Danis figured they hadn't forgiven him for rejecting Bartol's last appeal that he return to the fold. That took place when Danis was working for Bill Hughes. Looking like death warmed over, Bartol had taken the trouble to drive there in his Graham-Paige roadster and plead for Danis to go back with him. The boy proved he could be just as stubborn as Old Joe. Nor had the brother and nephew forgotten how he'd gone to the county attorney to report Bartol's abuse.

All Danis got from the visit were a few bone-bare facts: Bartol's lung condition had worsened, and his doctor ordered him to ride out the winter in sunny Arizona. Bartol traveled alone by train, but it was too late. He died a few weeks later at age fifty-nine.

■ ■ ■

Danis Vidmar bitterly regretted not going back to the homestead with Bartol that day. When pressed why, he couldn't explain it. All he knew was that it had gnawed at him for life. Danis was smart, but he was never good at articulating his feelings. In recalling his years with Bartol, he never once bad-mouthed the man, nor did he ever express happiness or despair over life's ups and downs. He was only comfortable presenting facts.

Maybe he loved the man but couldn't admit it.

He'd refused to oblige Bartol by calling him daddy, but in the end Bartol, not Luka, was the real daddy.

Maybe his regret was rooted in the hauntingly sad look on Bartol's face when Danis refused to climb into the big roadster.

Maybe it's because he sensed Bartol really loved him as a son and wanted him at his side when he died.

Maybe it's because, had he gone back, Bartol would have remembered him in his will. (As for Tomas, he'd left Bartol to work in a Roundup mine.)

Maybe, maybe, maybe … too many maybes.

If Danis couldn't nail the reason for his bitter regret, no one could.

8

SECRETS & LIES

At age thirty-four Maja Horvat was the proverbial stick in the mud. Born and raised by grandparents in the Slovenian village of Smolenje Vas, this homely peasant had never been anywhere in her life. And that was fine with her, since she'd become very set in her ways. Hers was a world so insular she'd never seen a banana.

Maja's parents abandoned her when she had been too young to remember them at all. She was left with maternal grandparents Anton and Urska Horvat, who were too old, infirm, and poor to raise her properly. The parents had taken off for America, with no plans to return. Because they didn't know where fate would lead them in that strange new land, they felt it was best all around if the Horvats adopted Maja.

The girl's father wrote her from time to time, sending her money and raising her hopes by suggesting he would send for her someday. Maja's mother couldn't write, having never been schooled, so she was as ephemeral as a ghost to the girl. And because the couple never owned a camera, Maja had no idea what they looked like. If the father had been serious about bringing Maja to America, two matters may have thwarted his plans. At roughly the time Maja would have been able to travel solo, just entering her teens, World War One erupted. And on the heels of war, Maja's homesteading parents were hit hard by Montana's devastating drought.

Maja wouldn't accept excuses. She wrote her father, "If you loved me, you'd send for me." She made a valid point since Anton, a drunk, died when she was seven, and time was running out on Urska, who hobbled about with a cane. And she was a harsh disciplinarian who frequently lashed the girl's fanny with a stick. She also worked the girl like a mule.

When Urska died, Maja moved in with the Brultz family across the dirt road, earning her keep by doing household chores and tending to a teenage boy and girl crippled by polio. Because there were no wheelchairs, petite Maja had to carry them about the livelong day; the hardest part was taking them piggy-back to the privy.

Still, Maja came to love the Brultzes because they treated her like family. She even gave them some of the money her family had been sending. But life was more than a workaday world because attached to the house was a tiny pub where neighbors gathered in the evening for beer and wine, and to dance the polka to live music. Maja's grandfather had been a regular, entertaining patrons with the clarinet. And Maja herself had become a whiz with the harmonica.

That Maja remained single might suggest she was a shrinking violet. On the contrary, she was an earthy, passionate woman, the kind no one ever wanted to get into a heated argument with. She loved to dance, and she wasn't a bit shy in singling out a man for a polka. She was so aggressive, opinionated, and temperamental that it's no surprise if men avoided her.

But Maja's other drawback was a long face with beady eyes, and a nose big enough to elicit gasps. She said her nose had been normal until age twelve, when some malady caused it to swell up.

But in 1937, Maja had been wooed and won by a handsome suitor ... or maybe it was the other way around. Joseph Kozamernik worked for a hospital in the nearby town of Novo Mesto. Slightly older than Maja, he still lived with his parents. In a studio portrait to mark their engagement, he seems meek and passive, perhaps the sort willing to let Maja wear the pants.

Maja never got over being abandoned by her parents, and fear of abandonment would plague her till her dying day half a century later. But with the Brultzes and Kozamernik, she no longer cared about going to America. She was happier than ever. Then a letter arrived from Montana that turned her world upside-down. For the past eleven years her brother had been writing her—and sending money—after the death of their father. He wrote that they were ready at last to send for her because Mother didn't want to go to her grave without ever seeing her girl again.

■ ■ ■

The Brultzes held a small farewell party for Maja on a Sunday in February 1938, several months after her brother's letter. Maja's cousin Ani, who remembered dining on pork and potatoes at the luncheon in the tavern, said it was more like a wake than a party. Everyone was teary-eyed knowing they'd never see Maja again. Even Maja wept. She told Ani she didn't want to leave but felt she had to obey her mother's will. Maja was from a time and place in which children didn't challenge parental authority.

What made leaving so deeply painful was that it ended her engagement with Kozamernik, whom she would never forget. The engagement photo remained with her for life.

Maja traveled by train to Cherbourg, France, where she boarded the *Queen Mary* with a third-class ticket. She was overwhelmed by this floating city of lights, especially since she'd lived in a village without electricity. She became seasick during a squall, with a Croatian steward telling her to go out on deck, look to the horizon, and breathe deeply.

Because she didn't know a word of English, her brother had employed the services of a company that met Maja at various points, beginning with Ellis Island. And the Travelers Aid Society kept the family posted, as with this telegram from February 22, 1938: "Maja arriving Roundup Thursday morning 4:21 Milwaukee Railroad."

The brother was waiting when the train pulled up to the clapboard depot. Then began the twenty-five-mile trip to the homestead over a badly rutted dirt road. The car's headlights revealed enough about this treeless terrain for Maja to feel an immediate dislike. Her spirits plunged even more as the car climbed up a knoll to a log cabin that looked poorer than anything in Smolenje Vas. Moreover, there was no village around for miles and no close-by neighbors. It was the middle of nowhere.

Maja had always heard that her mother had been a beauty at the time she left for America. But the figure that stepped from the cabin was anything but: portly, with badly weathered skin and a pained look that suggested a lifetime of hardship.

It was the face of Zalka Brodar.

■ ■ ■

At the dawn of the twentieth century, Martin and Zalka Brodar had been among tens of thousands of young adults who left the Austrian province of Slovenia for the capital of Vienna in search of a better life. He became an army gendarme (police officer), and she cooked for a wealthy family. They returned when Zalka became pregnant with Maja.

Martin at the time wasn't interested in fatherhood. He just wanted to immigrate to America. But he was broke. So he put some mighty big demands on the Horvats. He wanted them to rustle up the money for his passage. Then, after he was settled, Zalka could follow. The Horvats must have been thunderstruck when he told them they'd have to adopt the baby since there was so much uncertainty in his and Zalka's future. And the final jaw dropper: he would marry Zalka only in America.

Zalka may have felt powerless to challenge him, since he always had the last word. Moreover, she was getting up in years and still unmarried at thirty-three. She'd been with him for years and didn't want to lose him.

Throughout life Zalka would say it made perfect sense for the Horvats to adopt Maja. But the reality was that she was wracked with guilt for life. Long after Maja immigrated, a grandchild would remember seeing Zalka quietly weeping. When asked why the tears, she said it was on account of Maja.

■ ■ ■

That Maja Horvat kept her sanity in such a godforsaken place shows she had a backbone of steel. She was indeed her father's daughter. Since she had never driven a car (and never would), she and Zalka were totally cut off from the outside world. There never would be electricity in this remote area. It was as if Maja had been sentenced to Devil's Island.

What had started as an emotional reunion soon morphed into a living nightmare as the women became combatants. Maja was a fiery hothead like Martin. Normally passive Zalka could become a tigress when pushed too far. And Maja pushed her over the brink. Maja had her own ideas about how to run the homestead, and Zalka fought back because Stan decided these things. He frightened his mother so much she actually trembled while awaiting his arrival on Friday nights. Anyway, it was his property, because in the previous year he'd had Zalka, Albin, and Viv cede the land to him. And during his weekend visits, he would take the women to task for any shortcomings he detected in their performance. Sister Viv called him another Hitler. If Maja was a hothead like their father, so too was Stan, and the two locked horns like raging bulls.

Observing all this high drama was none other than Tony Vidmar, who had returned after leaving Joe Bartol. "Maja's arrival," he said, "was when the fireworks started." Tony was just biding his time now, with plans to return to the late Bartol's ranch, which now was run by nephew Paul Klobichar.

"Stan bring me here to be slave!" Maja fumed time and again over her brother's trickery. How true—he wanted to bring her over before Tony left.

Maja poured her grief in letters she wrote home, saying she'd go back to Slovenia if she had the money. Her misery was such that for the first time ever she began having outbreaks of eczema.

Stan poured more fuel on the fire by ridiculing her peasant clothing—the kerchiefs she wore wrapped around her head Gypsy-style, the heavy stockings, and the pointy-toed shoes. That really got under her skin, and what little money Stan provided her she used to buy the kind of clothing women in Roundup wore.

Maja's only solace was when sister Viv, with her two small daughters, drove up from Billings on weekends. Viv was so beautiful, charming, and sophisticated it was difficult to believe they were related at all. She tried her best to calm Maja, and she promised to help her transition into a culture that was totally alien to her.

Viv almost certainly encouraged Maja to focus her attentions on Tony Vidmar, who was ripe for the picking. At age twenty-four he was so shy as to be nearly invisible, and he'd never been with a woman before. Viv liked Tony a great deal, and she'd welcome having him in the family. They both had a great sense of humor and got along very well. She couldn't help but pity him because her mother and brother had exploited him in the worst ways. While anyone would have said Tony and Maja were a terrible match, Viv may have felt they'd both be better off if they were married. Otherwise, they had no future at all on their own.

Whether Viv played matchmaker or not, Maja felt short-timer Tony was her only ticket out of that hellhole. To hell with the age difference (she was almost twelve years older) or that they had little in common. She tried to worm her way into Tony's affections, but it didn't work.

On one of Merlin Vidmar's visits, Maja confided her difficulty. Merlin ordered her to bed Tony down in his cabin. Then all she had to do was lie that she was pregnant. Earthy Maja followed Merlin's advice, except for the lie.

As summer drifted into fall, Tony was ready to leave for the Judith Basin, but Maja didn't figure in his plans. Late in life she told others how she'd dealt with the matter. "I tell Tony, we need to talk. So we sit down on bench. And I look him in the eye, and he look me in the eye. And I say, 'Tony, I no got nobody, and you no got nobody. So let's be married!'"

They were wed in a civil ceremony in Billings on October 29, 1938. They wintered at the homestead and in the spring drove up to the ranch of Bartol's nephew. Tony herded sheep, and Maja cooked for the ranch hands, and often she didn't see her husband for days at a time.

She wanted out, and Tony satisfied her by landing a job at the Klein mine. When the Japanese bombed Pearl Harbor, he tried to enlist in the

Army but was turned down because coal production was deemed vital to national security.

A year later, Maja gave birth to James Edward. Tony, not she, had wanted a child. Although she doted on her baby, she made sure she'd never have another.

■ ■ ■

Maja's departure from the homestead presented a bitter irony. She'd ended up abandoning the mother who'd abandoned her. Zalka was furious, insisting Maja was making a terrible mistake marrying Tony, warning that he'd never be able to support her.

With Tony and Maja gone, Stan had little choice but to sell the property back to the government. As sole owner, he got to keep the proceeds. He used the money to buy a farm in Lockwood, a few miles east of Billings. Bizarrely, he moved wife Gladys, two sons, and Zalka there but remained in the coal camp, commuting on weekends. And he built a one-room hut for his mother since the two women didn't get along.

■ ■ ■

Strangers often mistook Maja and Tony for mother and son. The twelve-year age difference became greater as time went by since Maja turned matronly early on, while Tony retained his boyish good looks. But then, she treated him more like a son than a husband. She kept him on a tight leash and held the purse strings.

Friends and kin didn't recognize the stresses and strains in the marriage because Maja put up a good front. They only saw her smile, never scowl. She came off as a fun-loving lady who loved to entertain at home, serving up beer or tiny glasses of blackberry wine.

But with only Tony and James around, Martin Brodar's super-high-strung daughter was waspish, shrill, demanding, and opinionated. To challenge her on anything was playing with fire. James said he always felt like he was walking on eggshells. And Tony told his son that when she lit into him his innards would churn so bad he had to leave the house. But when he returned, as often as not she'd say contritely, "Honey, I be sorry."

When they married, they'd been two lost souls on the bumpy highway of life, not knowing where it would lead them. But at least they had each other to turn to for solace. And maybe that was good enough in 1938. But as the years rolled by, Tony knew that marrying Maja had been a mistake. After her death, he told James, "I never loved her."

9

HEART OF DARKNESS

In a 1931 studio portrait, Viv Brodar is China-doll lovely: powder-white skin, Cupid-bow mouth, eyebrows thin as antennae on a butterfly, marcelled curls that spill smartly down one side of an oval face that begs for cheekbones. At her side is fiancé Howard Olsen, who complements her with Prince Charming good looks, replete with lantern jaw.

Though their heads touch, one senses a disconnect. Howard forces a tight-lipped smile, while Viv looks as if she's waiting to see the dentist. There's something about her eyes that nags the viewer: their expression seems to shift from ingénue-soft to drama-queen-hard. A simple experiment, however, gets to the bottom of the mystery.

If each side of Viv's face is duplicated by placing the edge of a hand mirror directly on the photo, it reveals that Viv's eyes are not symmetrical. With the right side doubled to form a full-faced image, Viv looks like Snow White, eyes beaming with sugary sweetness. But with the left side doubled, she's now Snow White's nemesis, the Wicked Queen, eyes glaring with hatred. It's difficult to believe the two halves belong to the same person. If eyes are windows to the soul, Viv's are disturbing, hinting of a Jekyll-and-Hyde nature. In fact, there was a Good Viv and a Bad Viv. When good, she was considerate, charming, and witty; when bad, she was cold, unfeeling, and dangerous.

Viv's friends saw only the Good Viv, by far the most approachable of the ill-tempered Brodars. Even Tony Vidmar fell under her spell when he went to work for her mother at age twelve. Zalka and Stan treated the boy like a slave, not paying him for his labors and feeding him spoiled chicken. Viv, by contrast, was greatly sympathetic and served as a buffer. Five years his senior, she was like a big sister. She knew what it was like to be an only child on the homestead after Martin sent her brothers to board and study at a vocational school in Billings. She and Tony could privately ridicule Stan for being a tyrant and a buffoon. They were both fun-loving types with a great sense of humor. Over the years they became the best of friends, and Viv wrote him often.

Only Viv's husband and two daughters, Dolores and Lynn, saw the Bad Viv. Even Howard may never have seen Viv at her worst because she did her dirty work—against Dolores, never Lynn—behind closed doors at night, when he was away at work in the mail room of the *Billings Gazette*. Each evening without fail Viv morphed into the Wicked Queen, sadistically tormenting an innocent toddler who wept helplessly, paralyzed with terror as Viv struck her and screamed that she hated her. In short order, Dolores developed two telltale traits of emotional distress: nail-biting and bedwetting.

Viv's campaign of terror started soon after Lynn's birth, when Dolores was only four years old. Little by little she fancied Dolores was becoming more and more like Howard, a terrible thing to Viv because the marriage was on the rocks. Viv had married a man too much like herself—self-centered, independent, stubborn as a mule. A former coworker of Howard's remarked, "Once the guy made up his mind, that was it." That was also true of Viv.

Viv must have rued the day she'd met Howard, possibly at a weekend dance in any of several towns east of Billings. Viv, like Ania before her, was working as a factotum at the Klein boardinghouse, which a nephew described as "beneath her dignity level." With so little education and so few prospects, Viv was in a hurry to land a husband who could provide her with a better life.

Howard did indeed satisfy her material wants, from fancy satins and a fur piece to a Hoover vacuum cleaner and a refrigerator, when most neighbors were still using iceboxes and floor sweepers.

And while Howard was unaware of the terrible things Viv did to Dolores when he was away, he knew the marriage had been a mistake. After completing his night shift at the *Gazette* on summer evenings, he'd head to a lighted golf course, swatting balls clear into the wee hours of the morning.

One evening, when Tony and Viv went grocery shopping together, she told him to keep his eye on the butcher because he was in the habit of winking at her. Of course, Viv was a flirt who encouraged him. If she'd come to feel devalued in Howard's eyes, the butcher's attention raised her self-esteem. It was a lark to experience the kind of romantic sparks she'd once enjoyed with Howard.

During their occasional weekend visits with the Olsens, Tony and Maja could see Viv was treating Dolores too harshly, but what they saw was merely the tip of the iceberg. Maja once admonished her sister, which infuriated Viv. "Maja," she snapped, "you keep out of it! It's none of your business!" Feeling deeply sorry for Dolores, the Vidmars would sometimes take her to Klein for a weeklong stay. That suited Viv fine, allowing her to devote more time to her beloved Lynn, whom she fancied took after her, not Howard.

In addition to the beatings and scoldings, Viv threatened to send Dolores to a reform school if Howard should die. It wasn't that Dolores was bad or disobedient—she was just a child. And she didn't understand why her mother hated her. Looking back, as she approached her eightieth year, Dolores speculated that Viv had been jealous because she was Daddy's Girl.

Howard did indeed lavish the child with the kind of affection he no longer gave his wife. Little Dolores, not Viv, was the fairest of the fair.

Dolores would never forget the pain of growing up in a home that was right out of a gothic horror novel.

"She would lay me across the toilet seat and beat me with a wooden ruler while listing all the bad things I'd done that day, such as chewing my nails. Then I would be sent to bed while she and little sister would stay up and listen to the radio and make popcorn and fudge. This was daily without fail.

"From time to time she would put me in the bathtub, grab me by my feet, and turn me upside down to give me an enema.

"Because I was 'too fat,' I had to bend down and touch my toes a hundred times a day.

"Because she said I ate like a hog, she made me eat alone in the living room, seated at a tiny table facing the wall.

"She would put me in a baby diaper and make me stand in the living room with a hand mirror to watch myself sucking my fingers, which she'd dipped in pepper sauce."

And in between such events Viv would yell ugly epithets and strike and slap her.

Viv decided Dolores had to learn to play the violin. Each day she had to stand in her bedroom and practice for an hour. "If I quit playing, Mother would come in and smack me." Dolores said the family's tabby cat would lie on the bed and watch her. Dolores joked: "I could have sworn that cat was there to spy on me!"

"The only respite I had," Dolores went on, "was when Uncle Tony and Aunt Maja took me to their home for a week or so. How wonderful they treated me."

Since children take their cues from parents, it raises the possibility that the real reason behind Viv's cruelty toward Dolores was that she also had been abused as a child. If so, it had to be at the hands of Martin, not Zalka, with whom Viv had a most affectionate relationship. After all, Martin was such a hothead he once chopped Zalka's new stockings to ribbons because he felt she'd been too chummy with the traveling salesman. It's known that the three Brodar children greatly feared their father. Could it be that Viv had become her father? If so, Dolores was like a replica of Viv, whom Martin may have found endless problems with.

■ ■ ■

Viv's letter to the Vidmars, on March 3, 1943, was addressed to Tony, partly because she had a bone to pick with him and because Maja couldn't read English anyway.

> Hi, Toots.
>
> Yes, I do think it was about time you did a little letter writing. I wasn't going to write cause you never answer any way.
>
> At present Lynn is crying says that her tummy hurts. I dont know how much of that is put on, just started it this morning, yesterday she felt good.
>
> Your darling Dolores still chews her stubs and now she wets her pants too so I make her wear a diaper to bed every nite she also does it in school, so I made her wear it to school one day, and made her tell the teacher so she did, and the teacher told her that she is the biggest baby she ever saw to chew her stubs and wet her pants the teacher makes her sit in a corner in front of all the other kids for chewing her stubs and they all laugh at her, and she laughs with them now she has diapers and pants to wash after her own self as I am through washing such things. that's the girl you think so much of. then she talks about boy friends. I'll give her boy friends [her dirty diapers to wash]. Her report card shows that she sits sloppy and dont do her work neat in school. just like at home any thing she does its sloppy and has to do it 3 to 4 times over. sloppy stubs.
>
> And for me I dont feel a bit good. I've had a back ache for about 6 weeks steady day and night. I've been taking Di tetic treatments from the Dr. but they dont do me a bit good, only waist of money the Dr. says, the only way out for me is to have an operation. [Viv had already informed the Vidmars that the doctor advised a hysterectomy.] If the Dr. had his way about it I would

have it done last week all ready. but how I hate to think of it. it will cost about $350. I am afraid that it will hafto be done in the near future. Cause I can't stand this terrible back ache much longer. I also have lumbago to help it along. so you see I am in a nice fix. so dont be a bit surprised if you hear of me being in the hospital one of these days.

As for Grandma [Zalka] we saw her 3 weeks ago downtown [Billings] on a Sat. so went together to do shopping then she went right home on the bus, we asked her to come up and stay for a few days. but no she cant you know the farm [Stan's place in nearby Lockwood where she was living] can't go on without her.

Lynn just heaved so I guess she really is sick.

One of Gladys' [Stan's wife] calves froze. she didn't keep the cow in the barn while she was expecting her calf. so the calf was born up in the hills during the cold spell and froze. then Gladys put the cow in the barn after the calf was froze. but she didn't know any thing about it, she didn't know if it was all over with and mother told her, she said Gladys that cow already had her calf. you better go hunt for it that was after she kept the cow in [the barn] for about 4 days all ready. and sure enough they went looking for it, and found it froze. and she sure was afraid of Stan what he will say.

Well I guess you have about all the scandal I know. don't look for us over. not even Easter if I don't feel better. the Dr. is giveing me another therough exam this week.

You kids come on over any time you can. Give James a kiss and a hug for me. And write.

Just Viv.

■ ■ ■

Viv's undated follow-up letter to Tony and Maja:

Dear Kids.

Would of wrote sooner but I wanted to find out for sure when and how, and now its final. I went to the Dr. this afternoon for another exam. I am going to Deaconess Hospital this coming Mon at 3 P.M. and will be operated on some time Tuesday morning...

I sure went through hell this last week. Cant hardly stoop over my back hurts so bad and also my piles, they have been giving me hell to. so the Dr. is going to take care of them also & my pendix will be taken out. he said I am going to have quite an operation.

I got about 5 minutes of sleep. I just cant lay any way it hurts so bad. just about drive me nuts. I am in a hell of a shape...

I'll be in the hospital 12 days or more so the Dr. told me.

I'm sorry I or we wont be able to come down for Easter when you baptize J.E.V. and I would very much like to send him some thing but I just wont be able to as this operation is going to cost us more than we have, and they all would like to have cash you know how they all are...

And if I pass on you kids can take Lynn and raise her as your own and be good to her and I want her to have my big diamond ring and my crystals and wrist watch that's to be given to her when she is 14 or 15 years old. and Dolores can have whats left. Lynn would make a good pal for James cause their ages arent very far apart. and dad can have Dolores, she is his girl, and Lynn is mine. she is a little onry too but I love her. cause she is so sweet.

And I want to be buried in Roundup where there is enough room left for Mother so we can be together. so we can talk to each other, and keep each other co. so keep this letter until you see what happens. if I make it or not. as for my self I dont care. I have nothing to look forward to just the girls and thats all...

I'll bet you think I'm nuts, but all kinds of things can happen when the Dr.'s start cutting in to you, I'm ½ gone now the way I feel, so the other half wouldn't be hard to get rid of. ha! well so Long till we meet some where.

Recalled Dolores: "Just before she had her surgery she baked cookies so me and Dad wouldn't starve to death if she died."

And then she returned home to heal from the multiple surgeries. At first all seemed well. But two weeks later she was rushed to the hospital after she started to hemorrhage. The situation was dire. Since the Vidmars didn't have a telephone, Howard got in touch through Republic Coal. Tony and Maja rushed to Billings, but Viv was scarcely fit to receive visitors, and the pair were allowed to stay only a few minutes. Viv beckoned Tony to her side and whispered in his ear: "If I die it's Howard's fault."

A few hours later she was dead.

■ ■ ■

The Good Viv, the Bad Viv.

The Good Viv, fearing she might die during surgery, baked cookies so Howard and Dolores "wouldn't starve." But the Bad Viv demanded that the Vidmars make sure Lynn, not Dolores, inherited her valuables. And she had openly blamed Howard as she lay dying. Had he forced himself on her sexually when she was vulnerable to bleeding after surgery? Tony thought so.

Howard shocked the Vidmars during a visit when he bad-mouthed Viv. Then he rubbed his hands together in a symbolic cleansing gesture— he was happy to be rid of her. And he ignored her request to be buried in Roundup.

A year later he enlisted in the Navy Seabees, and the Vidmars took Lynn into their home, as Viv had wanted, while his kin accepted Dolores.

Maja disliked Lynn because she was mouthy, stubborn, got bad grades in school, and fought with classmates. Maja hit the roof when she witnessed Lynn prancing around nude in front of baby James. When Howard completed Navy duty she was much relieved to turn Lynn over to him, regardless of Viv's wish.

■ ■ ■

"At this late date," said Dolores, "I harbor no ill feelings toward my mother. I just wonder how she could have done those things to me. It sounds bad to say this, but I have always thought it was divine intervention that she died and did not live on to ruin my life; for I cannot say how I would have turned out if I'd had to put up with her through my teenage years.

"I once asked Dad if he did not know what was going on; he said he didn't know a thing. She did her dirty work after he went to work at night.

"And a child will never tattle and say, 'Mama beats me every night after you go to work.' Children do not operate that way; they think they are bad, and that is that."

■ ■ ■

Some years later tragedy struck the Olsens again. Seems Lynn had inherited Viv's dark side. One day she picked up a gun and fired a bullet into her head.

10

THE CRUELEST SNUB OF ALL

Young James Vidmar always looked forward to long Sunday drives with Mom and Dad in their old Chevy, going nowhere in particular. The trips weren't memorable, and James might have forgotten they took place at all had it not been for one particular drive on the rolling plains north of Roundup.

James, who was nearly five years old, remembered the outing started off in a most unusual way since Tony drove to Coal Camp No. 3 to pick up Aunt Lara and Uncle Pete. A half hour later, Tony slowed down and turned onto a long driveway, stopping at a two-story farmhouse. Everyone was strangely silent. Tony got out and went up the porch steps. The front door swung open, revealing a stout, potato-faced woman in her sixties with wire-rim eyeglasses. They talked briefly, and she shut the door.

Tony drove the car down a rough lane flanked by tall wheat, to a clearing where a stocky little man was tooling with machinery outside a barn. Wearing a straw hat and overalls, he gazed warily as the Chevy drew up.

Tony stepped out and took James with him. They walked over to the farmer. Tony said hi and asked if he was Kamil Balinski. Balinski nodded. Tony introduced himself and said, "You're my father."

"Who tell you that?" Balinski demanded.

Tony said it had been Ania when it was really Luka. She'd begged Luka never to tell Tony the truth.

What Balinski saw was a mirror image of himself. Both men were short, with fair hair, oval faces, prominent noses, and hefty chins. Balinski was bald down the middle, and Tony's locks were following the same pattern. The old man remained composed, but his innards must have been churning. It had been thirty-three years since he got Ania pregnant. After all that time, he must have felt his secret was safe. Making matters worse was that Tony had brought along an audience, and the adults in the car were gawking at him as though he were a freak in a circus sideshow. "No-no," he stammered, "no-no, I not be your father!"

Never the most articulate of men, Tony stood there a few moments in awkward silence. He then took his boy's hand, and they returned to the car.

■ ■ ■

Early one afternoon, several months later, there was a knock at the Vidmars' door. Tony had just left for work in the mine, and Maja was alone with James, who was on the floor playing with toys. She opened the door to a couple in their sixties. "Are you Mrs. Tony Vidmar?" the man piped up. "I be Kamil Balinski, and this be my wife, Veda." He wore a three-piece suit with a fedora; she was more simply attired, with a headscarf. Maja invited them to have a seat, but they turned down her offer of coffee. Veda gave Maja two jars of homemade pickles.

Kamil was disappointed Tony was away but said nothing to explain his visit. He said he and Veda had sold the farm and moved to Roundup. They then said goodbye, with Kamil encouraging Tony and Maja to visit.

■ ■ ■

Kamil Balinski was a secretive character with nary a close friend. Even Veda, whom he wed when they were both forty-two, was no soul mate. It was his first marriage, and it didn't end his womanizing ways. It was in

Butte, when he was working at the big copper mine, that he met Veda. She was married, with five children. Hers was a wretched life, with a husband who abused her and who spent time in a state mental institution.

It's not clear how Kamil and Veda became involved. Seems they were neighbors who happened to speak the same language, she being Polish too. Otherwise there was nothing about her that might have attracted a wolf like Kamil, since she was neither good-looking nor charming. The husband, distraught over Veda's involvement, threw himself under the wheels of a train.

Kamil and Veda were married in a civil ceremony in Roundup in 1927, and they bought the farm north of town. Theirs was a chilly union in which they behaved more like business partners than newlyweds. When Kamil made a big cattle sale, Veda demanded her share of the money. When he refused, she sued. They settled out of court. When they sold the farm, they split the money. Greed wasn't Veda's motivation; she didn't trust Kamil with money because he was a compulsive gambler. A bartender at the Moose Lodge in Roundup told Tony that in a single night Balinski lost twelve hundred bucks on the slots and punch board.

After the move to Roundup, Kamil went to work in the No. 3 mine. Well into his sixties, he should have been retired, but he was broke. After a long day's work, the last thing he cared to do was spend a quiet evening with Veda. Instead, he would walk the streets, visit the Moose Lodge, to which he belonged, or drop in on some female acquaintance in hopes of stoking the fires of romance. Old, fat, and bald, it's hard to picture him as a lady-killer, but he still had a way with women. Another pastime was visiting churches, to listen to the singing. And he loved watching the "holy rollers" at the Assembly of God church. He laughed heartily when he told the Vidmars the minister said to the congregation: "I know the devil is in here among us. In fact, I can see him! Look! That's him right there!" A man stood up and ran away.

After quitting the mining job, Kamil joined a road-repair crew at Yellowstone National Park. Seems he needed to get away from Veda as much as he needed money. At times he would take off in his Buick for parts unknown, leaving Veda high and dry for months. She was embittered and lonely. She and Kamil never had children together, and only one of her adult offspring still lived in the area.

If Tony and Maja visited her when Kamil was away, she'd rant and rave like a madwoman about his infidelity. She told them how she would wear disguises and trail Kamil when he visited lady friends. It took a while for the Vidmars to realize she wasn't insane.

Tony and Kamil had hit it off when they got together for the first time in Roundup. Not only did they have the same farming and mining background, they both shared a robust sense of humor. Amazingly, the paternity issue didn't come up, not then, not ever. But Balinski came close to an open admission. One evening when the Vidmars visited Veda, she handed them an invitation to Kamil's birthday party.

"I have to tell you something," she said slyly. "I ask Kamil if he want to invite you to party. He say 'Sure, go ahead.' So I start to write, and I say, 'How you want me write this? Do I say Dear Tony or Dear Son?' He say, 'Make it Dear Son.' So I start to write that, but he say, 'No! Better make it Dear Tony.'"

The Vidmars and the Balinskis got together about twice a month. Socializing always precluded the presence of other Vidmars. Had Kamil come to the Vidmar home and seen cars parked there, he'd have driven on.

James recalled an amusing incident when the two parties were visiting Yellowstone. When Tony pulled into a gas station, the attendant remarked on how much Kamil and Tony looked alike. He asked if they were father and son. Both broke out with shit-eating grins, lying through their teeth.

■ ■ ■

Thirty-three years into their marriage, Veda died of leukemia, and Kamil rushed into another union at the ripe old age of seventy-five. The old new bride lived in Missouri, which is where the pair settled, if such a word can be used, since Kamil abandoned his wife the way he had abandoned Veda, taking long solo trips in the Buick. The Grim Reaper tailed him on the last of his travels, delivering the mortal blow in Thermopolis, Wyoming, where Kamil indulged in the rejuvenating warmth of one of the town's famous hot springs. His body was found floating in the water.

The Vidmars never learned the cause of death. James speculated that his heavy wine intake and his diabetes caused him to black out and drown.

Seems his widow had had enough of him, since she didn't want to bring the body back to Missouri. He was buried in Thermopolis.

Although Balinski had told Tony, "When I die you be first to know," his son learned of the death from the weekly *Roundup Record*.

And so the old man went to his grave without ever saying the words his boy so badly wanted to hear, "Tony, you be my son."

11

FROM SUDDEN DEATH TO SPOOKY VIOLENCE

Perhaps the most gruesome and haunting tragedy at the Klein mine was the mysterious death of Frankie Fortune, Stan Brodar's brother-in-law. It was especially sad because Frankie just then was happier than ever, having just married sweetheart Marge Harper.

"Such a nice young man," recalled John Miklich, a pump operator at the time. "Sort of happy-go-lucky, but quiet."

"He was my buddy—a real nice guy," said coworker Red Murray, a ruddy-faced Scott, traveling six decades back down memory lane. "We did all our drinking together. Used to go down to his dad's cellar and tap those wine kegs," luscious full-bodied reds Mr. Fortune had made.

On Saturday nights the two pals would drive to a dance hall in Cushman, boozing and schmoozing in the parking lot and getting "pretty well oiled," Red added.

Young toughs couldn't resist picking a fight with Red, who was cocky and loud as thunder.

Red laughed, "Frankie and I often had to fight our way home!"

Frankie's coworkers were green with envy the day he drove a shiny brand new black Chevy into the camp.

"How proud he was of that car," said Miklich. "Always kept it clean and shiny."

Prouder still was Frankie of his new wife Marge Harper, who worked in the Klein boardinghouse, a factotum like Ania Vidmar and Viv Brodar before her. They'd eloped just days before the tragedy, tying the knot in Green River, Wyoming. The reason they did it that way was because the Slovenian Fortunes were Catholic, and Croatian Marge was not. The Fortunes had badgered Frankie so long and hard to break up with Marge that he moved in with a friend. Then, with no more ado, Frankie and Marge sped down to Green River in his shiny new Chevy to begin a wonderful new life together.

There's a photo of the two in front of the car. Frankie looks crisp and assertive in a three-piece suit and fedora. Marge is plump, with a round face, short straight hair at the sides, and a pile of curls on top. Miklich said they were a perfect match, since she was just as fun-loving and happy-go-lucky as Frankie.

When the couple returned to Klein, they stayed with Frankie's pal.

On the morning of January 9, 1941, Frankie kissed Marge as he headed out the door, on his way to the mine.

"Honey," he said, "when I get off work, we're going out and buy ourselves some furniture."

Frankie, like so many people from that period, kept his money stashed away in a secret hiding place, since so many banks went under during the Great Depression, and customers lost their life savings. Frankie planned to withdraw money from his hiding place after work, so he'd be able to buy whatever Marge liked at Wier Furniture. He'd never told her where he kept the money, and when he started to do so, she cut him off, saying it could wait.

Frankie was a handyman at the mine, and one of his duties was firing up the boilers so miners would have hot water when they showered after work. Another was lubricating the cables that lowered and raised the cage that transported miners and coal. The cables rode on two huge pulleys located in the derrick-like tipple, which looked like a tin shed situated over the shaft. Frankie did the lube job between 11:00 and 11:30, when the cages were idled during the lunch break. Frankie scaled the steep tipple staircase, entered the tin enclosure, and commenced with the lube job.

At 3:30 Red Murray and coworkers completed their shift and piled into the wash room but were puzzled that the water was cold as ice. If there was a problem with the boiler, Frankie surely should have notified a supervisor. The men rushed out to find out what the hell was going on. None wanted to go home covered from head to foot black with coal dust.

The response they got was blank stares. Somebody may have seen Frankie climb up to the tipple, but no one could recall him coming down. As word went around, miners shook their heads when asked if they'd seen Frankie. Well, he sure as hell wouldn't still be in the tipple for a job that took a few minutes.

Frankie's friend Stanley Cebull figured he'd best go up and check anyway. So he climbed up as miners gathered around in suspense. Only seconds later a visibly shaken Stanley made his exit. When he touched ground supervisors got the story first. Then one of them ordered that the mine's whistle let out four shrieks to indicate a serious accident had taken place.

Meanwhile, Frankie's father had been unloading coal cars directly beneath the tipple. Like everyone else he was concerned but figured Frankie would show up with some excuse. He went on with his work until the whistle sounded. Red Murray remembered the sudden horror on his face as he dropped the shovel and cried out in despair, "Oh God! It's Frankie!"

■ ■ ■

The *Roundup Record* described it thus:

> Frank Fortune became entangled some way in the cable and sheave wheel and was killed. His right arm was cut off at the shoulder, there was a fracture at the back of his head, and he was cut badly about his back and head. There were no witnesses to the accident and possible causes are merely conjecture. Cause of his death could have been the skull fracture or he could have bled to death.

Authorities and officials of the mine, however, could advance no definite cause for the accident, and it was decided not to hold an inquest.

Mutual grief didn't end the rift between the Fortunes and Marge. As the parents saw it, the marriage was illegitimate in the eyes of God because it had been a civil service ceremony. But they were dealt a terrible blow when Roundup's Catholic pastor refused to conduct funeral services because Frankie had married outside the church. They were so angry they never set foot in the church again.

Grieving Marge refused to believe Frankie had been careless. She went so far as to assert that someone had started up the cables in order to murder Frankie. It might seem believable in an Agatha Christie novel, but not in real life, at least not in Klein. Red Murray and others rejected Marge's story as far-fetched. One thing they were all certain of: Frankie didn't have any enemies. Marge packed it up and left Montana.

As for that hidden money, it was never found.

■ ■ ■

Frankie's buddy Red had a terrifying brush with death that resulted from a conflict with miner Steve Pecherich. At age fifty-six, Pecherich had worked at the No. 2 mine for thirty-six years. He'd immigrated from Croatia in 1909, when he was seventeen, and spent time in Illinois, where he may have worked in a mine. In 1912, at age twenty, he came to Klein. "He was a small, hard-looking guy of about five-seven," said one old-timer. "He had a dark complexion and a full head of hair. And he was quiet. Really quiet. Didn't associate with anyone."

Pecherich was the polar opposite of brassy and sassy Red Murray, who had a hell of a sense of humor, which Pecherich lacked altogether. The pair only got to know one another because Red had a crush on the miner's daughter Alice. That was in the late 1930s, when Red would walk Alice home from high school. They dated for a while, but the romance ended when Alice told Red she could never marry him if he didn't go to college.

Red had long planned to become a miner just like his dad. Much as he loved Alice, nobody was going to tell him what to do. But the two remained good friends.

Red had never been close to Alice's dad, but he said, "We had a good relationship. I never had a problem with him."

After high school, Red saw combat in World War Two, and by 1948 was a seasoned miner. He should have known better, but one day he told Pecherich he might go after his job. It was a joke, but Pecherich didn't get it. Red considered Pecherich's job the most boring one at the mine. The man spent his days at a tiny sub-station where alternating current was converted to direct current, which is what was used in the mine since it made the locomotives (coal cars) run more efficiently.

Red wanted to earn as much money as possible so he could one day buy a ranch. So he began working weekends at another post. It made Pecherich so jealous he rounded up two coworkers, and they complained to the boss that he should have informed them about the job so they could have applied. The boss decided they could all take turns at Red's weekend job.

Red was madder than a coiled rattler. He stormed over to Pecherich and his cronies and yelled: "I don't know why you pulled this crap! It's not your business to ask for my job! No more than it's my business to ask for yours!"

Red then gave the boss a tongue-lashing, reminding him he was breaking union rules. He said if others did that job he'd still have to be paid. The boss meekly rescinded his decision.

Red's weekend job involved disposal of coal-rock tailings. The material was loaded onto train cars and taken to a spot about a quarter of a mile from the mine. There, via a chute, it was transferred to trucks that hauled it off into the hills.

Much of the detritus ended up on the ground. That's where Red's job came in, operating a front-load tractor to push aside the tailings so trucks could get in and out. Locals did the rest, salvaging the tailings for their coal stoves.

Working the front-loader is what Red was doing the afternoon of October 8, 1948. As he went about his work he was in mortal danger, but he didn't have a clue. Within seconds the life of this big brawny Scot might have been snuffed out, like a candle in the wind, had it not been for a small boy.

Six-year-old Dick Rorick had wandered alone from home to watch what to him was a great big toy in action. Dick was observant, and a forest-green Buick sedan drew his attention away from the front-hauler. The car had parked a fair distance off, on the main roadway, but there was nothing there to explain why the driver did so. Dick's eyes remained on the car, waiting to see what the driver would do. He watched in amazement as a rifle protruded from the window.

"Hey, mister!" Dick yelled at Red, who had trouble hearing, what with the front-hauler's noise. "Mister, look! That man in the car! He's got a gun!"

The word "gun" registered, and Red saw Dick pointing to the car.

"The second I saw that gun," Red said, "I threw myself down under the steering wheel."

He was suddenly plunged into a living nightmare. He knew that forest-green Buick. And he knew the owner. And he knew the gun—a 30.06 deer-hunting rifle. On several occasions he'd been at the Pecherich home with Alice when Steve came driving up in the Buick with the carcass of a deer strapped to the hood.

Red began trembling, shocked that Pecherich, who he'd thought was a friend, had only one aim in mind: to kill him, as though his life was worth no more than that of a deer. Red was no elusive deer; he was a sitting duck. It was just like in the war, when he rode atop a tank across Europe, from Le Havre, France, to Wolfgang, Austria. Armed with a .30-caliber machine gun, his job had been to protect the tank. He'd survived fierce combat without a scratch. And now here he was atop a front-hauler but without a machine gun.

Pecherich fired, and Red heard the bullet zing above his head. Now he knew what it was like for a terrorized deer when it knows it's being stalked. Red leaped and hit the ground running as fast as his legs could take him. Not fast enough when he could hear bullets whistling past. He danced a crazy zigzag, expecting to be hit any second because Pecherich was no novice when it came to guns. Red ran toward the camp's houses a hundred yards away. He flew up the steps to the first house he came across, that of Dusty Stamp and his wife.

The Stamps had heard the shots and seen him running frantically their way, and their door was open to receive him. "Call the sheriff!" he screamed. "It's Pecherich! He's trying to kill me!" Luckily the Stamps had a phone, which many other houses lacked. Dusty put through the call, then retrieved his rifle. The trio watched from a window as Pecherich started up the Buick and headed to his own house.

They watched Pecherich step out of the car with the rifle, enter the garage, and exit without the weapon. He entered his house. Within seconds he emerged with a .22-caliber rifle, and he began walking toward the Stamp house. Red ran off for the post office, where a crowd had already gathered, including Red's dad, who handed him a 30-30 carbine.

Pecherich stopped at a narrow but deep ravine that carried water runoff from the mine. He could have jumped across, but he just stood there a few moments before returning to his house.

By the time sheriff's deputies arrived, twenty hair-raising minutes had elapsed from the time of the first gunshot. Pecherich stationed himself on the back porch, rifle in hand. When lawmen pulled up to the house, Pecherich yelled not to come any closer. He then placed the barrel to his temple and blew his brains out.

The *Billings Gazette* reported Pecherich had committed suicide, with no mention of his attempt to shoot Red Murray.

Red was fit to be tied when the Roundup paper called it a "gun battle." He stormed into the office and raised hell.

At least a hero emerged from this ugly event: none other than little Dick Rorick. He'd saved a man's life.

■ ■ ■

Maja Vidmar described down-and-out types as "beaten people." That's the term she'd have used for next-door neighbor Nick Colletti, an Italian immigrant who'd worked in the mine for decades. Now in his sixties and retired, he lived in squalor in a one-room shack whose interior was a smelly, cluttered mess, with walls blackened from the coal stove and Nick's pipe smoking. He stank even more than his hovel since he rarely bathed or washed clothes.

He habitually peed his pants as he stumbled home in the late afternoon after getting tanked at Fay's Bar down the road. Watching from a window, Maja would laugh, telling son James it looked as if snails had crawled up and down his legs.

He was a loner, and if he had pals they were the drunks who sometimes picked him up in a car on the way to Fay's, knowing he'd pick up the tab. Nick was proud to do so. If they asked if he had the dough, he'd wave a wad of bills in their faces and boast, "I got lossa money!"

The Vidmar and Colletti houses featured much yard space in between, divided by a wire fence. Maja loathed Nick but tried to be friendly if they were both outside, with her hanging up clothes to dry and Nick fussing with his garden patch. Unlike judgmental Maja, Tony had a soft side for beaten people, and he tried to be kind to Nick. He'd call out, "How's she goin', Nick?" and, if not hung over, he's say, "Pooly goot, Tony, pooly goot." But if under the weather, he'd cry, "South America!" If feeling really chipper, he'd chirp, "Fine and dandy!"

But Tony could never engage him in much conversation.

Tony and Maja's perception of Nick as a harmless old man ended scarily one day. It started while Maja was hanging clothes on the line and Nick was digging a long trench between his garden and the fence. When Maja asked why, he shot back: "I be mad at Tony!" Pointing to Vidmar trees, he cursed, "Goddama trees! Roots come over! Kill my garlic! Kill my onions! You tell Tony I mad at him!"

He completed the trench, filling it with sharp objects, such as broken glass and razor blades, which he seemed to think would sever the invasive tree roots.

When he returned from the mine, Tony was greatly disturbed by Maja's account. He felt he'd better go at once to settle the matter, but Maja was scared and tried to talk him out of it. Tony brushed her aside, certain Nick wouldn't harm a fly. He knocked on Nick's door, but Nick hadn't returned from Fay's Bar. With the sun starting to set, Tony decided to wait outside, with James at his side riding a tricycle. Neighbor Jerry Vessel came along and stopped to chat. His interest piqued, he decided to wait with Tony.

Nick soon showed up, stumbling badly, even having trouble as usual opening his yard gate. Tony and Jerry rushed him, which may have caused the old man to react with blind instinct, as though he were being attacked. He whipped out a knife and seized Tony's neck with his other hand. Before Jerry could grab Nick's arm, the blade sliced across Tony's neck. When Jerry pried the knife from his hand, Nick continued on to his front door.

Maja rushed over in hysterics, and James began to bawl, and there was blood everywhere. Jerry and Maja rushed Tony into the house and sat him at the kitchen table, going through a pile of towels to soak up the blood, desperately hoping for it to stop. Luckily, the blade had missed the carotid artery. Jerry was about to drive to the sheriff's office, but Tony stopped him. He believed whatever was eating Nick would blow over.

But the Vidmars were so badly shook up they decided to get away for a few days. They drove to Bellingham, Washington, where Tony tried but failed to get hired at a coal mine.

While away, someone had tipped the sheriff, who visited Colletti. But no one learned the outcome of the meeting. The tipster was none other than Kamil Balinski.

Tony not only forgave Nick, he made a practice of going to his house, taking James along, to cut what little hair was left on the old man's bald pate. And he continued to greet Nick. "How's it goin', Nick?" And Nick would smile and say either "Pooly goot, Tony, pooly goot," or "Fine and dandy," or "South America!"

12

ROSARY BEADS & BOOZE

Klein was the pits for Paulina Kobec, who lived a few houses down from the Vidmars. The widow shared her crumbling shack with two of her seven adult children, Lizzie and Teddy. Nothing had gone right for Paulina and Gregor Kobec after they'd immigrated from Slovenia. On the other hand, as adults, the other five children had moved to Washington and California and become very successful.

It's difficult to figure out how a family of nine managed to get by in so tiny an abode, which featured a crammed kitchen, living area, and only one bedroom cut off from it by a curtain. By the 1940s, when the Vidmars became acquainted with the Kobecs, the house was in dire need of repairs. But Paulina couldn't undertake them because she was destitute. Her only income was county welfare. The two live-in children were hardly any help. Lizzie sold Real Silk hosiery door to door, often traveling around the state by bus. (The Kobecs never owned any cars.) And Teddy was a slow learner who never held a full-time job.

Paulina earned a reputation as the biggest crybaby in all of Klein. Engage her in any conversation, and she'd shift the topic to Poor Me, I no have this, I no have that. Maja, however, suspected Paulina had lots of cash, which her children provided. Maja seethed with anger whenever she looked out her window and saw a welfare officer heading toward Paulina's place.

By 1912 the Kobecs were settled in a coal camp at Aldridge, Montana, just north of Yellowstone National Park. In a book on that historic town, Paulina and Gregor appear unidentified in a photo in which a dozen people are lined up in front of a log cabin, which may have been a saloon run by Gregor and a brother. Gregor is roguishly handsome, with twinkling eyes and a bushy mustache, holding high a beer mug. Paulina has a big, round, plain face that resembles that of England's future Princess Margaret.

The coal soon played out, and Aldridge became a ghost town. The Kobecs moved to Klein, where Gregor built that tiny abode, with an attached saloon. And Paulina had seventh child Teddy. Then the Kobecs experienced the worst bad luck. In 1918 Montana enacted Prohibition, two years before Congress made it the law of the land. Gregor turned the saloon into a pool hall that became a hangout for teenage boys, and he went to work in the mine.

Rumors circulated for the rest of Paulina's life that while Gregor was in the mine, she and his brother were having a hot and heavy affair.

By the time the Vidmars got to know the Kobecs, Gregor had died, and the other children had already left the state. Paulina's house was in such disrepair that the out-of-state children paid Tony to put up a new roof.

Paulina actually complained that Teddy was running up her electric bill by playing his radio.

James loved when he and his mom visited Paulina, who would sit them at the kitchen table and serve delectable treats. She was a first-rate cook, and savory aromas always filled the house. She fixed a wonderful saffron chicken soup, and her sweet-roll bread *potica* (poteetsa) was a knockout.

Maja, who was still learning how to cook, spent much time discussing recipes and techniques with Paulina. And much as she loved sampling Paulina's dishes, she became alarmed by how many long strands of gray hair ended up in the food. James recalled how she once told Tony, "I no like eat there—always find hair in food!"

Maja became increasingly critical of Paulina, and one bone of contention was the old woman's drinking. Anytime they visited Paulina, they always found her with a glass of orange juice in one hand, rosary beads in the other. Maja was certain the OJ was laced with booze. To Maja it was hypocritical to carry on like a devout Catholic while drinking heavily the livelong day. After all, why should God help a drunk who gave equal weight to rosary beads and booze?

Maja may have hoped Paulina would replace Zalka as a mother figure, since the latter had failed in that department. In fact Maja seldom saw her mother, and the antipathy between the two was mutual. James remembered a roaring row between the two when he was a toddler.

But if Maja hoped she'd get tea and sympathy from Paulina, she was sorely disappointed. Paulina could hardly fill that role when she saw herself as the most pitiable figure in the camp. In a photo of the two women, one notes a disparity in living standards. Maja looks glamorous in a long rabbit-fur coat, with her stringy locks transformed into marcelled curls. Paulina looks as if she'd just stepped off the boat; she's wearing a drab sack dress and bib apron. Together they look like *nouveau riche* with the hired help.

But Maja did try to help the Kobecs by taking them to Roundup when she and Tony shopped. The Kobecs, however, were too demanding, wanting to be driven here, there, everywhere. Maja told Tony: "Dey ask too much! We no be taxi! Give Paulina a finger, she take whole arm!"

Paulina's out-of-state children came to the rescue as Paulina became more and more infirm with age. They brought her and Teddy to live in California. Lizzie remained put, making a barebones living selling hosiery. Pretty and vivacious, she never married. Even if she was interested in men, she scared them away with her eccentricities.

One example of her odd behavior was the night she burst into the Vidmar home on a mission. She was after Tony, who'd become a Catholic (in name only) before he and Maja had a second, church wedding. Lizzie prodded Tony to see a priest at once and confess his sins so as not to burn in hell for eternity. When Tony gave her a flat-out no, she begged him to confess his sins to her so she could relay them to a priest.

Lizzie lived into her nineties, and after her death the house sat abandoned for a couple of decades, enclosed by a jungle of weeds, bushes, and vines. A next-door neighbor acquired the leaky ruin and razed it.

13

BEATEN PEOPLE

The time: June 1956.

The setting: an aging three-story brick building in downtown Great Falls.

A tall sign juts out from the façade with vertically stacked letters that spell OXFORD HOTEL.

Owner Elsie Taylor hasn't had any luck selling it.

Small wonder. It's a flophouse.

What's more, she doesn't own the building, only leases the two upper floors. The two dozen or so rooms are mostly vacant.

Asking price: five grand, which in 1956 might buy a fully loaded Caddy.

Elsie plans to retire when she gets that five grand. Meanwhile, the hotel is also home—a two-room suite facing Central Avenue. Rooms to either side of the building face dark and narrow alleyways.

Presently, a turquoise and white Dodge with fins parks outside. Out steps her agent, with a husband and wife and their teenage son. The agent ushers them through a central door and up a wide staircase. They make a U-turn at the landing and head directly to Elsie Taylor's humble suite. The door opens, and the agent introduces his client to Tony, Maja, and James.

■ ■ ■

This was a momentous event for Tony, who'd dreamed for years of some-day becoming his own boss. He'd recently undertaken two business ventures. First, he tried to sell women's hosiery, the result of reading an ad in a men's magazine. One customer called the hosiery the worst she'd ever worn.

Then he invested $750 in napkin-and-menu holders that he installed in restaurants. They allowed patrons to deposit a penny through a slot, pull a lever, and learn their fortune. The message would appear behind a glass panel. However, a short time later Montana passed a law deeming such a device illegal because users did not get a printed message.

Tony then turned to Joe Bartol's nephew Paul Klobichar. With his mother's passing, Paul had inherited Bartol's ranch, and he'd turned it into a lucrative enterprise. He also became a real estate agent and the owner of an apartment complex in Great Falls. One day Paul mailed Tony a note saying the Oxford was a sweet deal. Never mind that his firm had listed the property.

Tony's brother Danis said late in life: "I figured if Paul had anything to do with the Oxford, it wasn't any good. He was the kind of agent who'd tell a seller his price was too high and make him keep lowering it. Then, when he got it where he wanted it, he'd turn around and buy it himself! I told Tony, 'You can't trust Paul. He's a good talker, takes after Old Joe. He just wants his commission!'"

■ ■ ■

From the moment he'd heard his dad talk about the Oxford, James began dreaming of the delights of living in a real city. But now he finds the Oxford depressing beyond belief. He's troubled about the communal bathroom he'll have to use and the likelihood of roaches hiding out in the cluttered basement.

Although Maja shares her son's misgivings, she's reluctant to object since she knows nothing about the business, and her English is so poor she can't follow the talk between Tony and Elsie. She only hopes Paul Klobichar was right to urge Tony to buy.

Elsie is a chatterbox who tends to go off topic. James will always remember one of her digressions.

"One day this man called on the phone, wanting to speak to so-and-so. There was no one by that name living here, and I said, 'Mister, you've got the wrong number. This is the Oxford Hotel.' He hung up and called right back. 'Mister, I just told you no one by that name is staying here.' He asked if I was sure. 'Sure, I'm sure,' I said, 'I own the hotel!' Well, he got real huffy and said, 'If I've got the wrong number, why do you keep answering?'"

■ ■ ■

Tony borrowed a truck to make two trips to Great Falls hauling furniture from Klein, even the refrigerator. The family then left together in their 1950 Buick. On a lonely stretch of highway the car struck and killed a doe deer. "It was very depressing, like a bad omen," James said. "It put a damper on the rest of the day."

Tony and Maja moved into Elsie Taylor's apartment, and James took an adjacent room. He was given the family's new TV, with a fishbowl black-and-white screen. He hated the place, which didn't feel like a home at all. What really bugged him was the communal bath, and the flush toilet, since he'd grown up using the privy. When Maja mentioned this to Elsie, she declared, "Why, Maja, he needs to be housebroken!"

With each passing day Tony's heart sank lower and lower as he realized the Oxford was shaping up to be the biggest mistake of his life. He hadn't anticipated how much work it took to keep the place humming. Too poor to hire a chambermaid, he did all the work himself. But Maja never offered to help, which bugged him. One day he came across a mattress soaked with menstrual blood. In a letter to sister Lara he called the place a pigpen.

Maja told James their tenants were all "beaten people." One drunk who was in arrears with rent pleaded with Tony to give him time to find a job. Tony agreed, only to discover one day that the man had absconded. When Tony tried to quell a noisy dispute between a drunken couple in their room, the husband screamed from behind the door, "Go piss up a rope!"

Tony was sure Elsie Taylor had cheated him, replacing new linens with old threadbare ones after he'd inspected the inventory, before the sale. He believed she'd given the new merchandise to a brother who ran a local motel.

Tony dropped in on Paul Klobichar at his office to unload his problems, but he got the cold shoulder. Danis had been right about Paul.

James believed the stolen linens were only one of several instances of Elsie's deceit. Tony saw an attorney who urged him to demand a full refund on the sale or else he'd take her to court. Tony had a face-off with Elsie, and she was so frightened she caved in. She wept when she wrote him a check for five grand.

Tony was totally at sea about what to do since he didn't want to return in defeat to Klein. What's more, Klein's mining days were numbered now that Milwaukee Road trains had converted almost entirely to diesel.

Although Maja had loathed semiarid Musselshell County upon arrival there in 1938, she'd come to love the place, so she was happy to return. Meanwhile, she wanted to go to Salt Lake City to visit an old friend from Slovenia. Leaving their possessions in storage, they headed there, and Tony drove around in circles for a few days, desperate to find work, ranging from construction to warehousing. Supervisors right off asked him which Mormon Church stake he belonged to. Answering in the negative, he was told there were no jobs.

Tony got his mining job back, and he bought a house. Because he wasn't an easy man to read, his son never could decide how big a blow the failure of the Oxford had been. Perhaps Tony didn't suffer the keen disappointments that most people do because he'd grown up in such abject poverty that he never developed great expectations in life.

Just a few weeks later Republic Coal announced it was halting operations for good. Ownership passed on to a superintendent, but only briefly. Soon the pumps quit siphoning the ever-intruding water, and the miles and miles of tunnels soon flooded. Other area mines, whose coal didn't provide fuel for trains, fared no better. Mine No. 1 east of Roundup had closed, and No. 3 barely outlived No. 2.

The Vidmars stayed put for two more years, until they could find a buyer for their house. They then bought a quaint little place in Roundup that had once been a schoolhouse; it had been moved to the present location, a tree-studded neighborhood just a few blocks from Main Street. Over the years Tony held a variety of odd jobs, working for the railroad, mine No. 3, and for a company that laid electrical lines across the treeless plains. He did brief stints as a garbage collector and helping brother Danis, who'd married into a farm family and ended up as sole owner. He even worked on the massive Yellowtail Dam, which meant commuting to Roundup on weekends only.

■ ■ ■

Roundup declined sharply with the closure of the Klein mine. And matters went from bad to worse when the Milwaukee Road went belly up in 1980, which meant no more rail service. The railroad pulled down the old depot and removed miles and miles of tracks.

Roundup, which in its heyday was dubbed "Miracle City on the Musselshell," had become but a shadow of its glory days, with too many empty shops on Main Street. Tony badly wanted to move to Billings, which had overtaken Great Falls as Montana's biggest city. But Maja wouldn't hear of it, even though son James lived there with his family. He worked as an editor at the *Gazette*.

Tony also had a hard time talking her into making a trip to Slovenia, which he was eager to see. When he told her he'd go alone, she changed her tune fast. For Tony to do such a thing, well, that smacked of abandonment, and Maja never, ever got over her fear of that. It had spooked her when Tony was away at the Yellowtail Dam. She actually feared he might meet a woman and never come back.

Tony allowed her to boss him around on too many counts since he just wanted to keep the peace. As he once put it, his stomach would churn when she went into a rant. But there were times he put his foot down and did what he wanted, such as buying a new car when he craved having one.

The pair began to suffer serious health problems, ranging from Tony's diabetes and recurring heart attacks to Maja's decade-long bout with cancer. With her days numbered, she insisted that Tony remarry, saying he was too young to remain single. She cared deeply about him as though he were her child.

Tony took her advice. Only a year after her death he married widow Emma Neumann, of Lockwood. He was seventy-three, she a year older. They were a near-perfect match, both imbued with a zest for life. Their previous mates had been overly domineering, and now they were free to enjoy life to the fullest. Tony had endured a life of hardship and disappointments, but fate provided him with a happy final chapter. Emma was the best thing that had ever happened to him.

Their happiness was cut short three years later when Tony suffered a fatal heart attack at their home in Billings. Ironically, it happened on Thanksgiving Day.

■ ■ ■

Late in life Tony bought Maja a most unusual gift. James, returning from Air National Guard duty in Texas, was startled when he spotted a doll perched on Maja's bed. That was so unlike her. She'd always had a strong distaste for the kind of knickknacks that abounded in sister-in-law Lara's house, calling them dust catchers. But Tony's gift had thrilled her beyond words because it was the first doll she'd ever had. As a child she'd envied little girls who had dolls, something her grandparents were too poor to give her. Tony knew it would make a perfect gift.

Tony and Maja didn't leave behind anything that could be called heirlooms for James and wife Karen to take into their home and treasure. The only object that filled the bill was the doll.

After more than half a century that little dark-haired cutie hasn't aged a day. Apart from an eyelid that no longer opens and closes, she isn't the worse for wear, either. Her colorful outfit is neither faded nor frayed. She wears a robin's-egg-blue bodice with a green-and-blue floral bib, whose colors and pattern are repeated in the skirt. Her waist is cinched with a pink sash.

She isn't a collectible. Tony likely found her in a variety store. But James and Karen know they can't part with her.

How could they? She was, after all, Maja's little girl. She was the first thing Maja saw in the morning and the last thing when she turned out the lights.

James and Karen just couldn't abandon Maja's little girl, the way Zalka abandoned Maja.

14

LAST MAN IN THE MINE

Musselshell County's strangest miner was Johnny Nelan, a mysterious figure clad in black from head to toe. At the No. 2 mine he was in charge of the pumps that kept the miles of underground tunnels from flooding. He had the graveyard shift, but he loved it. After all, he had neither family nor any social life.

Old-timers laughed at what an odd duck he was, but they were fast to point out how friendly and smart he was.

Johnny Nelan was of medium height, with a big round ruddy face, high cheekbones, and piercing eyes. He loved chatting with anyone about anything, but he lit up like a light bulb if the topics were mining, mechanics, hunting, or travel. He always spoke wistfully about his desire to see Alaska. But after moving from Illinois to Musselshell County, he stayed put for his remaining fifty-one years, never venturing any farther than Billings. He spent most of his free time in Roundup, hitching a ride there or waiting on the highway for the Greyhound bus.

Johnny Nelan revealed little about himself, and if anyone pried he'd snap, "None of your business!" He was such a miser that some people enjoyed teasing him, asking who he was going to leave his money to when he died. "To folks who mind their own business!" he'd retort.

Because he never cooked, he never used the coal stove in his one-room shack—not even to heat the hut on the coldest of winter days. He endured subzero nights in a sleeping bag. Although the shack didn't have running water, he always kept clean, showering in the mine's wash house at the end of each shift.

Johnny came to Montana in 1909, when he was thirty-one, following a fiery disaster at a coal mine in Cherry, Illinois, where he worked. He moved into his tiny shack, which was in the backyard of a man named Charles Cornish, whose wife was said to weigh 400 pounds.

Young John Miklich lived in the neighborhood and came to know Johnny since he often visited the Cornishes, whose son was a good buddy. Thirty years younger, the boy was drawn to the strange miner because he was so bright and well-informed on most any subject. The two spent countless hours chewing the fat, but not once did Johnny ever invite the boy into his abode. When Johnny bid Miklich goodbye, he'd open the door just the barest crack and slip in. Johnny influenced the youngster greatly; many years later John Miklich would also become a pump operator.

No employee was more dedicated to Republic Coal than Johnny Nelan, who happily worked seven days a week until the forty-hour work-week became standard. And he loved double shifts. Whenever the company needed him, he was there. He was such a company man that when he bought war bonds, he named Republic as beneficiary.

Unlike miners who kept Klein's many saloons in business, Johnny never touched a drop, nor did he smoke.

He carried three watches at all times: One was five minutes fast, one five minutes slow, and one right on time. Once, he even chartered an airplane in Billings to get to work after missing the Greyhound bus.

Because he worked the graveyard shift, Johnny wouldn't be up and about until noon. By mid-afternoon he'd take the Greyhound to Roundup for his one meal of the day, at the Bungalow Café. After giving his order, he'd add emphatically, "You can double that." When it arrived he'd reach for the ketchup and pour it over everything. Then he'd lick the bottle top clean before replacing the cap. After packing away all that grub, he'd order a milkshake. That was his only meal of the day. He once told Tony Vidmar, "You just spoil yourself if you eat more than one meal a day."

When he left the café, the waitress always cleaned the neck of the ketchup bottle.

The first thing Johnny did when he arrived at the mine was gulp down an enormous amount of water. That way he could go an entire shift without another drop.

Johnny was deferential to coworkers, and he amazed them all with his formidable intellect. It's doubtful if there was a better-read individual in all of Musselshell County. He always had magazines stuffed in his black jacket.

He never spent money on himself, but he could be generous with people he liked. If a coworker happened to mention a tool he needed, Johnny might surprise him with it as a gift. Once, John Miklich's mom asked Johnny if she could borrow Mrs. Cornish's fruit jars since the family was away. Johnny turned her down flat. He would never take anything from his landlord's house. The next day a cabbie pulled up to the Miklich house with dozens of fruit jars that Johnny had bought for her.

Many years later, when John Miklich and wife Dorothy drove to Roundup they often gave Johnny a lift. Each time he'd press them to accept payment, which they refused. He sat in back with the couple's daughters—Romalie, Rosemary, and Antoinette—and each time he surreptitiously gave them ice cream money, up to five bucks. John and Dorothy would take turns declaring, "Johnny, stop that!"

In 1956, at age seventy-eight, Johnny was still working when Republic Coal closed the No. 2 mine. Even after the other workers ditched their hard hats, Johnny was needed to man the pumps while equipment was removed. That kept him busy for the better part of a year. But it must have been hard on him when he rode the steel cage for the last time. After all, that rat maze had been his real home for half a century.

Johnny spent his remaining years visiting Roundup most every day. By then he was living in a company shack, about four hundred yards from the highway. He'd walk down the coulee to Highway 87 and wait for the Greyhound bus, which came along around nine o'clock. He'd spend the day walking up and down Main Street, visiting with shopkeepers, gabbing with acquaintances he bumped into, and pigging out on his mid-afternoon meal.

He loved hanging out at Kibble-Kase Sporting Goods Store, which had been the Swastika until World War Two. Owner Hap Kibble had been a professional baseball player. The store had a soda fountain and magazine rack that brought in the kids. Kibble shooed away those who came to read but never buy.

The lounge area featured a leather-upholstered mission-style bench where old-timers hung out. Herb Ottman said Johnny was often there holding court, opining on endless subjects. Herb had never conversed with the old man and couldn't imagine doing so since Nelan was so stern-faced, gruff, and creepy-looking, dressed in black and wearing an old cap with a bill.

Herb was among the many teen boys who dropped by just to peruse the girlie magazines. One day, while feasting his eyes on a nudie-cutie, he was embarrassed when someone from behind placed a heavy hand on his shoulder. This time it wasn't Hap, but Johnny Nelan, staring down at him like the Wrath of God.

"You don't want to look at that trash!" he thundered. "It's no good for ya, I tell ya!"

Nelan reached for a copy of *Popular Mechanics* and thrust it into Herb's hands.

"Read that instead! It'll do ya good!"

He led the boy to the cash register, paid for it, and sent him on his way.

Another time, Herb was standing in front of a display case full of knives, his gaze riveted to a wicked yellow switchblade. It wasn't that Herb needed a knife. It had more to do with image in the age of Elvis, ducktails, leather jackets, and gangs. Oh, wouldn't he look cool showing off such a weapon to school chums. As he drooled over it, ready to ask Hap Kibble to unlock the case, he suddenly heard that voice behind his back.

"You don't want to buy that!" Johnny boomed. "Steel's no good! Won't last!"

Johnny then singled out a ho-hum pocketknife only an old fart could lust for. He talked nonstop about what a fine piece of work it was, with a tempered-steel blade that might last a lifetime—unlike that tawdry yellow number that was garbage in Johnny's book.

Herb returned later for the sexy yellow number.

In movie westerns cowboys and Indians expertly hurled knives whose blades never failed to sink into their targets. In his backyard Herb placed the blade between two fingers, stretched back his arm, and hurled the weapon at a tree.

Ouch! The knife slammed into the tree and fell to the ground. Herb was aghast! The blade had broken in half!

The Bungalow Café had been Johnny's favorite eatery because it also served as bus depot. But by the time he retired, Greyhound had switched to the Arena Café, and so did Johnny. The Arena also had a section devoted to sporting goods, books, and other merchandise.

It was there, in 1956, that seventeen-year-old Ed Moss struck up a friendship with Johnny Nelan.

It began one day while Ed was browsing paperback books. With no introduction, Nelan came up to him and said he was an atheist. Ed didn't even know what the word meant and was speechless. Johnny explained the meaning of the word, and Ed was shocked that anyone could be such a thing. Why, everyone believed in God—even the devil! Johnny rambled on and on, jumping from one topic to another. Ed remembered he spoke slowly, in short, declarative sentences that were so stilted he thought Johnny might be a foreigner.

Ed found himself so enraptured by Johnny's observations that he began hoping to run into him.

Greyhound drivers were so accustomed to picking up Johnny each morning that if he wasn't standing by the road they'd actually wait awhile until he showed. If he didn't, they'd sound the alarm at the Arena Café, urging someone to go check up on him.

He died in the spring of 1963 at age eighty-five. It's believed all his money went to some grand-niece, even though he wasn't close to kin in Illinois. Old-timers recall that when two nieces once visited him, he wasn't at all pleased. They were on their way to the West Coast, and he made it clear he didn't care to say more than hello, goodbye.

There was also speculation he might have buried his money near the shack. Herb Ottman and his dad combed the land with a metal detector, but nothing turned up. They did get a surprise, however, when they lifted a trapdoor to the cellar. The floor was covered from wall to wall with old flashlight batteries, a half-foot deep.

There was a time when most everyone in the area could talk about Johnny Nelan. But most folks who remembered him best, such as Herb Ottman and Ed Moss, have passed away. Today, Johnny's grave in Roundup is as neglected as one would expect. However, on Memorial Day one might find flowers on it, courtesy of some kindly individual. A nice touch, that: flowers for Johnny Nelan, last of the old-time miners. And a good old soul to boot.

Printed in Great Britain
by Amazon

69679005R00066